The Biltmore:
Beacon For Miami

The Pickering Press Florida History Series

Broadway By The Bay: Thirty Years at The Coconut Grove Playhouse
The Early Birds: A History of Pan Am's Clipper Ships
The Biltmore: Beacon For Miami
Children and Hope: A History of The Children's Home Society

The Biltmore:
Beacon For Miami

Helen Muir

The Pickering Press

The Pickering Press
2665 S. Bayshore Drive, Suite 601, Miami, FL   33133

© 1987 by The Pickering Press
All rights reserved. Published 1987
Printed in Great Britain
92 91 90 89 88   5 4 3 2

Photo Credits: pp. 18, 33, 35, 53 (courtesy Historical Association of Southern Florida); pp. 38, 40, 49, 57, 59, 81, 90, 91,
102, 103 (courtesy The Miami News); pp. 41, 42, 51, 61 (courtesy Gleason Waite Romer Collection, Miami-Dade Public Library); pp. 9-11, 13, 14, 47 (courtesy Fishbaugh Collection,
Department of State, Florida Archives); pp. 27, 29 (courtesy
Mrs. George Merrick); p. 50 (courtesy Jack Ott); p. 73 (courtesy
Mrs. Hillard Willis); p. 71 (courtesy Sam Beneckson); pp. 96-98
(courtesy Norman Fine).

Library of Congress Cataloging-in-Publication Data

Muir, Helen
   The Biltmore : beacon for Miami.

     Includes index.
     1. Miami Biltmore Hotel & Country Club. I. Title.
TX941.M5M85 1987   647'.94759'38   87-10807
ISBN 0-940495-05-8
ISBN 0940495-04-X (pbk.)

Front cover illustration by Martyna Kupciunas

Contents

You admire this tower of granite weathering the hurts of so many ages. Yet a little waving hand built this huge wall and that which builds is better than that which is built.

Ralph Waldo Emerson

About the Author

Helen Muir is the author of MIAMI USA, a history of the area published in 1953 and still in demand by book buyers today. She has written for national magazines such as the *Saturday Evening Post, Nation's Business* and *Woman's Day*. Mrs. Muir came to Miami in 1934 from the *New York Journal* to direct publicity at the Roney Plaza Hotel and since then has written columns for both the *Miami Herald* and *Miami News*, served as children's book editor of the *Herald* and drama critic of the *News*. For three years she wrote a syndicated column from Miami. She plays an active role in the field of libraries. In 1984 Mrs. Muir received the Trustee Citation of the American Library Association for, among other reasons, "her eagerness to spotlight the library at every opportunity." That year she was elected to the Florida Women's Hall of Fame at ceremonies at the Governor's mansion.

An Introduction

T HE first time I heard the Miami Biltmore mentioned I was sitting in the patio of the Westchester Biltmore Country Club in Rye, N. Y. surrounded by attractive men. Howard Chandler Christy, Russell Patterson, and James Montgomery Flagg were all famous illustrators at that time, which happened to be late Spring of 1934.

They were not paying me court. I was on business bent, gathering material for a *New York Journal* newspaper column I was then writing.

We were having cocktails. There was candlelight. However, I was not the sole woman present. For the first time I was encountering the beautiful and vivid fashion writer Prunella Wood, who by her own admission, "had a long standing love affair with Coconut Grove." It was also the first time I heard Coconut Grove mentioned.

When she spoke of the Biltmore being in Coral Gables, I asked the obvious question. Why, since it was placed in Coral Gables, was it called the *Miami Biltmore*?

Because, I was told, Miami carried more weight as a dateline. Today, thanks to television and the wildness of current events. *Miami* is synonymous with *Vice* , and *Coral Gables* falls more gently on the ears of city fathers and developers alike. Now, in all its literature in the Year of Our Lord 1987 the management of the exquisitely restored Biltmore chooses to re-introduce this grand old hotel as *The Biltmore of Coral Gables*.

So be it.

Still, I submit (and I am more than ever assured of the fact after undertaking research for this small book) that you can take Miami out of the Biltmore—but you will never take the Biltmore out of Miami.

The Biltmore is more than a magnificent hotel for visitors from around the world. It is a gathering place for special events within the community. It is loved by the people to a high degree.

But we have personal business back at the Westchester Biltmore in the Spring of 1934.

The scene has returned to me often in the ensuing years. I had no idea as I sat there that by late Fall that same year I would be writing for Carl Byoir Associates with offices at both 42nd Street and the new Waldorf Astoria. My assignment was to publicize the third annual Miami Biltmore Fashion Show and Supper Dance for the benefit of the Goddard Neighborhood Center, which was being held that December at the Waldorf. I was then to proceed to Miami Beach to direct the Roney Plaza Hotel public relations.

Eleanor Roosevelt headed the Invitation Committee, debutantes modelled the clothes and, I learned immediately, the name of Mrs. Henry L. Doherty was never intentionally omitted in any releases sent to newspapers. Her husband owned the Miami Biltmore, the Roney Plaza, and the Key Largo Anglers Club, all faraway names to me but which later would figure as part of daily life.

I was slated to leave for Miami Beach a few days after the event at the Waldorf. The wind whistled up and down Park Avenue as I darted back and forth between those two offices, carrying a small black fur muff to keep my hands warm and all the while wondering what it would be like in Florida. I had no intention of making this more than a temporary stop and, in fact, was considering a job offer in Persia.

The night of the Miami Biltmore Fashion Show and Dinner Dance, it snowed. The men in my party had to remove their top hats in order to put chains on the car as we travelled to hear Emil Coleman and his sixty piece orchestra play "My Silent Love" for the first time. It was still snowing the night I left New York after having been given a farewell dinner which almost caused me to miss the ten o'clock train.

I had dreamed of traveling by boat on the Clyde Mallory Line but was told it would take too long. As it was, I spent two nights sleeping aboard the Florida East Coast train called *The Havana Special.* It was early morning when I stepped down at the old Florida East Coast station and for the first time in my life *saw* sunshine. Entering that early morning light was then and has remained one of life's choice experiences.

I was met by Jane Buck and Odie Monahan of the Byoir staff and driven in an open roadster to the Miami Biltmore. It struck me as a curiosity, rising from the pancake-flat terrain, sort of all by itself, almost a mirage.

We had breakfast in the patio, where caged birds twittered as I received my first assignment. No time to change clothes, I was told. I was due immediately to interview Captain Eddie Rickenbacker at the Roney. He was back from Chicago and the successful eight hour fourteen minute inaugural flight of *The Florida Flyer*.

We met at the Cabana Club of the Roney where the clothes I was wearing were unsuitable, consisting as they did of very high heeled black velvet slippers and an ankle length crepe tunic dress with long sleeves (in a fashionable color that season known as jungle green!), the same dress I'd worn at the farewell dinner my friends had given me.

Rickenbacker elected to walk on the beach as we talked. Those velvet shoes sank into the sand with every step until he realized what was happening and we sat down.

A few years before he died we sat down again, this time for family Christmas Eve dinner, and reminisced about our first meeting.

My first grandson was permitted to ask for the flyer's autograph. As he obliged, Captain Eddie turned to me. "You got sand in your shoes," he said. It was the old Damon Runyon quote and meant of course that I had stayed in Florida.

That would not have happened had not the *Miami Daily News*, as it was then called, telephoned me as I was packing to return to New York.

Would I please come in and help them out on rewrite since they were shorthanded?

In those days "the season" ended shortly after George Washington's Birthday and it was still snowing off and on in New York. So I said yes.

My byline was Helen Hansl and it appeared on feature stories and film reviews. Overnight I became church editor and introduced a weekly food broadcast over radio station WIOD which the Cox newspapers had purchased. With each new task sug-

"Ralph (Pop) Willets, chief photographer of the Miami Daily News *snapped this picture in front of the News Tower in the Spring of 1935. We were on our way to the Miami Biltmore to cover the National PTA Congress for the* New York Times. *That evening I met Bill Muir."*

gested by *News* editor Allan Cass, my paycheck grew. It was the newspaper's way of encouraging me to stay on.

On April 17, 1935, my picture appeared on page one interviewing Mrs. Harry E. Wright, whose son, Victor A. Wright, was the engineer officer aboard the first official San Francisco to Honolulu flight by Pan American Airway's nineteen ton flying boat, the *Pioneer Clipper.*

Having me broadcast spot news was considered a forward move by the newspaper, and the quick jump from city room to broadcasting studio was accomplished by the simple act of taking the elevator to the News Tower.

In addition, I covered occasional stories for the *New York Times* and wrote a *Universal Service* column, so in a twinkling I had been transformed into a Miami based newspaperwoman.

My friend Floyd Gibbons, who landed in Miami Beach that summer, insisted I would stagnate if I stayed in Miami and urged me to return to New York. He himself fell so in love with the place he purchased a North Bay Road bayfront home.

I interviewed him on the air and told him I'd think about his offer to have me go to Ethiopia as a war correspondent.

Actually there was another important decision to be made. I was being romanced by an eligible bachelor who was Carl Fisher's lawyer, played polo, and recited poetry. His name was Bill Muir. In August I decided to return to New York and figure out my future. This time, as a free agent, I took the boat.

For my first glimpse of Manhattan after eight months of being away, I stood in the bow of the vessel. While it was in the process of docking, I observed two men pacing up and down, passing each other as they did. Both were wearing white suits.

Certainly one was Father—but the other? . . .

It was Bill Muir. He had flown up to help me come to a decision.

My father and my future husband were strangers, about to be introduced.

A whole new life was opening up and in a matter of five months I would have a new byline. It would be mine for more than half a century.

Helen Muir
Coconut Grove

Birth of the Biltmore

NOBODY ever said that the Florida land boom of the 1920s was anything less than an American dramatic event or that Miami was not the center of the building explosion following World War I. Even the *London Daily Observer* paused to point out that "there is something happening in Florida that is very significant and very real."

Real was not exactly the word being used by American bankers as they saw their depositors streaming toward Miami and environs in a frantic rush to purchase land in a get-rich-quick movement that caught fire and burned with schemes both wild and wonderful.

It was against this backdrop that the Biltmore Hotel was conceived by a young creative genius named George Edgar Merrick, who turned a family truck garden into a grand hotel in the European tradition.

He waited until he had created a city, first planned in every detail on paper, and named Coral Gables after his family's home. Unabashedly, he advertised it as "The City Beautiful" and "The Place Where Castles in Spain Come True." It was part of what was being called "The American Riviera" or in more realistic terms "The Master Suburb."

The first mention of this grand hotel was splashed over the front page of the *Miami Daily News and Metropolis* on February 19, 1924, at which time the boom was in its ascendancy and Merrick was riding high.

The newspaper described a country club to accompany the hotel which would cost a quarter of a million dollars. Dues would be three hundred dollars a year and the initiation fee was set at fifteen hundred dollars. Membership would be limited to three hundred.

Martin L. Hampton had drawn plans for the spread. It was estimated that the hotel would be built at a cost of $1,250,000. There would be 350 rooms in the hotel which would have a high tower, an architectural adornment that fit into the Merrick overall plan from the beginning.

The next news bulletin concerning the new hotel and country club came in a grand manner on November 25, 1924, when he invited two hundred influential Miami businessmen to attend a dinner at the Coral Gables Country Club to introduce his new partner in the project, none other than John McEntee Bowman, top man in the hotel field. With Bowman came his own architects, Schultze and Weaver.

Earlier the general construction manager for Coral Gables had given out population figures indicating summer residents numbered twenty-five hundred. In the winter the figures jumped to thirty-five hundred. These were offered as proof that the need existed for a "great hotel . . . which would not only serve as a complete hostelry to the crowds which were thronging to Coral Gables but would also serve as a center of sports and fashion."

Bowman's getting into the deal was a plus all the way around. Dr. Allen Morris, the distinguished Florida journalist and historian, a fledgling reporter in Miami in the early days, looked back on the scene:

"The Bowman name provided cachet for that fairyland out there where plans for gondolas and canals and riding to hounds might be causes for snickering. The Bowman name gave it credibility and was a sign that the Biltmore was going to be for real."

Bowman was the daddy of a string of Biltmore hotels, the first of which opened in New York City on December 30, 1913. It was followed in 1922 by the Westchester Biltmore Country Club, Rye, N. Y.; next came the Los Angeles Biltmore. In between, in 1919, Bowman purchased the Henry B. Plant hotel, the Belleview in Clearwater, added the name Biltmore, and thus made his entry into Florida hostelries.

Henry Plant had acquired thousands of acres in the Bellair and Harbor Oaks districts of Clearwater, for the site of his hotel. It was his son, Morton Plant, who recognized the dawning craze for golf and installed two eighteen-hole courses. *Life* Magazine described the fourteenth hole on the East Course as "one of the Great Golf Holes in America." One senses echoes of this hotel in the matter of the two eighteen hole golf courses planned for the Miami Biltmore.

Future caddies for the Biltmore Golf Course with their mentor, Mr. Hirsch, owner of a Biscayne Boulevard furniture store.

It was said, that during the late 1800s "as many as fifteen railroad cars were parked at one time on the hotel's special siding," for the industrial magnates of the day who came to relax. George Merrick didn't have a railroad siding, but he had buses rolling in from all over the U.S.A. with the name Coral Gables plastered over them and real estate offices shouting out the name in Chicago, New York, Atlantic City, Pittsburgh, and Washington, D.C. A huge sign in the middle of Times Square made the name known to New Yorkers.

Merrick was the first of the big time Florida developers to employ the use of advertising on the national scene and the *Saturday Evening Post, Vogue* and *Forbes Magazine* were frequent vehicles for this purpose. The creator of The Master Suburb was proving himself to be a master publicist.

Who would have thought to invite William Jennings Bryan, to act as pitchman for the sale of Coral Gables real estate? The three times candidate for the Presidency of the United States, Secretary of State under Woodrow Wilson until he resigned because of his anti-war principles, would stand and sometimes sit on a platform at high noon in the middle of the Venetian Pool ("the most beautiful pool in the world").

It offered The Great Commoner something of a change from his outdoor bible classes conducted in Bayfront Park and, then too, provided a piece of extra "change" in the form of one hundred thousand dollars a year for his services, half of it deliv-

Men and mules make golf courses.

ered in cash, half in land. No piker, George Merrick. He paid it out for two years. In addition Paul Whiteman provided the music for these noonday events.

The creation of Venetian Pool and Casino indicated a spark of genius in itself. When a big hole was created after all the rock was cut out of the earth for the initial house building, it was turned into a picturesque swimming pool to provide the setting for all manner of exciting events. It was designed by Denman Fink and Jeanne Biegger, who later married Dean Martin, was crowned an Orange Bowl Queen there.

The night of that dinner when Bowman was introduced to the town folks, he congratulated Coral Gables for being elected as a site for another hotel in his chain and announced this new one would cost ten million dollars to build.

Leonard Schultze, partner in the architectural firm of Schultze and Weaver, rose to outline the "three golf courses, polo fields and tennis courts" that would be part of a spread that would be divided into two parts: a country club and a hotel. The term "sport house" was used to designate the physical attractions that would be available.

Ground breaking ceremonies for the Miami Biltmore. Left to right are Marcel Gotchi, hotel manager, Carl Byoir, Charles Flynn and William Jennings Bryan.

Not yet in service were the Venetian-striped gondolas for the canals Merrick was digging to get access to Biscayne Bay, where he planned to build a casino and bathing facility as well as a hotel to accommodate a thousand guests. The Biltmore capacity was a mere "400 rooms and suites, each with a private bath."

The day of the groundbreaking for the Miami Biltmore took place in March 1925 and there were no superstitious doubts about it being Friday the 13th. Who could doubt the performance of George Merrick, who in a few short years had become a legendary figure? Who could doubt the Florida boom?

The Biltmore would be the "tallest building in Florida" at 315 feet with a curved ramp to lift it up off the flat pineland for a grand entrance above street level.

At the last minute an extra inch was added to the plans—just in case.

Charles S. Flynn, the fellow who brought Merrick and Bowman together, officiated at turning the first shovel full of earth. He had gained an amusing title, "the steam engine in boots," on the jobs of supervising the building of the Sevilla Biltmore in Havana, Cuba and the Atlanta Biltmore.

George Merrick was not alone in his appreciation of towers.

Miami, along with other parts of the nation, was mad about towers, and by the time the Biltmore opened on January 15,

1926, after ten months of round-the-clock activity, there were three of them. You could stand in the Tower of the Roney Plaza at Miami Beach and gaze across Biscayne Bay to view the Tower of the *Miami Daily News and Metropolis* and then beyond— clear out to Coral Gables where the Biltmore Tower gleamed.

One way or another, they were all patterned after the fifteenth century Giralda Tower of Seville, Spain— and small wonder. The same team of Leonard Schultze and S. Fullerton Weaver had drawn the plans for all three of them.

Neither had ever been to Europe nor had George Merrick, but they were followers of the Beaux Arts movement which had become highly fashionable following the 1893 Columbian Exposition in Chicago.

Moreover, Schultze had been associated with the firm of Warren and Wetmore in working on the design for Grand Central Station, and Whitney Warren actually had studied at the *École des Beaux Arts* in Paris. As indicated, the idea of introducing towers to the landscape was not limited to Miami.

The Terminal Tower in Cleveland, Ohio was created before the Biltmore and, in fact, is still standing. The Madison Square Garden Tower in New York City was not so fortunate. It was being destroyed about the time the Biltmore was being constructed. They too were adaptations of the Giralda Tower of Seville.

While George Merrick had not traveled in Europe, he had visited Mexico and Central America and had long ago decided that a Spanish type architecture was the most suitable for the sub-tropics so, by the time the Biltmore was built, this style was very much in evidence under the description "modified Mediterranean." What Schultze and Weaver introduced into the Biltmore were dashes of Moorish and Italian flavors to whet the appetites for opulence exhibited by those who frequented the Bowman hotels.

It was a high old time for grand hotels. A new kind of rich, many of whom had built fortunes during World War I, were in avid search of opulency and elegance in one package. The Biltmore was created to fulfill these appetites, but it would do more.

The lights in the Giralda Tower would guide wayfarers by land and sea and air and become a strong symbol for generations, even during a forty-five year period when the impressive

Skeleton of a grand hotel.

structure was used for hospital purposes and later abandoned to vandals.

The beautiful Roney Plaza is gone, bulldozed in 1968 and replaced by a nondescript apartment house. The Tower fought back, forcing the wrecking crew to postpone the final demolition overnight.

The *Miami News* Tower, renamed Freedom Tower during the influx of Cubans in need of government assistance, remains a wreck with constant unfulfilled promises of restoration. As of this writing, a new hope is being held out, the owners claiming that investors from Saudi Arabia are standing by ready to put up $8.5 million to buy it. Since 1979 the crumbling News Tower has been listed on the National Register of Historic Places. Not long ago the dynamic former Miami Mayor Maurice A. Ferre proposed buying it for ten million dollars and turning it into City Hall.

Of the three towers the Biltmore alone stands tall, its beacon once again visible to travelers from all over as airplanes come to land at one of the world's busiest airports. The Biltmore story is a drama, an American drama with continuing themes, the most recent as grand as resurrection.

A plain listing of the cast of characters making entrances and exits over six decades would almost fill this book. A few will make their appearances as the story unfolds, then disappear.

The making of the Biltmore, summer of 1925.

Others like George Merrick will remain throughout.

The centenary of his birth on June 3, 1886, went largely unnoticed except for a brief ceremony at City Hall, but by sliding in just before 1987 the restoration became a fitting celebration for the man whose dreams were large and not exceeded by his ideals and principles.

There was a vast difference between George Merrick and some other developers of the period in that he was not led by a desire for quick riches so much as the strong need to create beauty.

Merrick wrote poetry and surrounded himself with qualified individuals to help carry out his dream of putting into place on this earth a community so beautiful and well balanced and filled with order and significance that it would stand as a model before the world.

Before the first lot was sold, he had prepared a skeleton of his intentions and set down stiff building restrictions. His city would have a college, schools, churches, a library, and a profusion of planting and architectural flourishes including plazas and graceful entrances.

His favorite song was "I Dreamt I Dwelt In Marble Halls"—and for a time he did. The fact that the land boom coincided with his plans and accelerated them before sweeping them away entirely is one of life's ironies.

George Merrick actually invented Coral Gables, and the Biltmore hotel was his child. There is no way to separate them.

Nor can the story be told without the Merrick family and how they came to South Florida and planted the seeds that resulted in both the Gables and the Biltmore.

We'll start at the very beginning, which was the blizzard of 1895 that hit New England.

Long Ago and Far Away

G EORGE Merrick always wanted to be a writer and began scribbling poetry while a boy.

He was nine years old when the blizzard hit the Massachusets village of Duxbury where the Merrick family lived.

This is how Merrick, the man, recalled it:

"All New England was in the grasp of that terrible blizzard of 1895, the thermometer was far below zero. There had been over forty pneumonia deaths in the old Cape Cod village within the week and as many lay at deaths door nearby our parsonage home where death too had just visited."

Death had visited and taken off Ruth, Helen's twin and George's baby sister. The father, Solomon Greasley Merrick, an ordained Congregational minister, and his wife, the former Althea Fink, coped with their grief, the blizzard, and Solomon Merrick's beleaguered flock as well as the remaining children.

George Edgar, their first child, was born in Springdale, Pennsylvania and was eight when they arrived in Duxbury from Solomon's first church in Gaines, New York, where he served for seven years. Their firstborn, who seemed solemn and occasionally diffident in public, was in the bosom of the family a high-spirited prankster given to impromptu wrestling. Then there were Ethel, Almeda (called Medie in the family), the twins, and a second son, Charles.

Solomon and Althea Merrick were remarkable people by any standards.

Althea was a painter and head of the Fine Arts Department of Lebanon Valley College in Annville, Pennsylvania, which is where she and Solomon Merrick met as fellow students.

Althea's father was a circuit riding Methodist preacher who served congregations in Pennsylvania and Ohio and who never

Meet the Soloman Merrick Family of New England. That is son George with his bicycle. He would grow up to build a city called Coral Gables

used anything but three initials as a signature. Even in the family bible he was The Rev. H.G.G. Fink on all occasions. He also made considerable money in a patent medicine which caused high amusement in the family. He was a pronounced prohibitionist, but it was whispered that the content of the elixir was all of ninety-eight percent alcohol, something of which the Rev. Mr. Fink appeared blissfully unaware.

After their marriage, family devotion was as real as love of beauty for both Althea and Solomon Merrick. His forebears were Scots who settled on the Eastern shore of Maryland, and from them he had inherited, along with high intellect, a quiet gentleness but a steel-like determination. He studied at the Yale Divinity School to prepare himself for a life of service in the church.

The two were able to create a particularly happy home life for their children, with Althea being noted for always finding time to stop and play in spite of her household duties and continuing interest in painting.

These were cultivated people, and humor played an important part in the creation of a family atmosphere which at the same time was staunchly upright.

Living through the crisis of the blizzard and Ruth's death, Solomon Merrick continued to search in his mind for an answer. Surely there was a more rewarding way to bring up a family in a happier clime? His answer came in the person of an old friend who had just returned from Florida.

Let George Merrick tell the story: he came "with veritable Marco Polo tales of a wonderful new fairyland of enchantment around a newly planted town on Biscayne Bay.

"No greater contrast could be imagined than that between those tales of enchanted sunshine in the South and the frigid scene of ice, desolation and death all around Cape Cod. That evening my father definitely embarked on an undertaking, which in connection with all his circumstances, traditions, previous living and environment, called for the same courage, steadfastness of purpose and will power as fired Columbus on his adventure from Palos into the Great Unknown."

Understandably, working out the details of such a radical change in living required time but Solomon Merrick never wavered in his determination from that moment on. He began a steady search for a new home. When found it turned out to be what would become Coral Gables.

Steered by the Rev. James Bolton of the Union Chapel in Coconut Grove, later Plymouth Congregational Church, Solomon Merrick purchased for the sum of $1,100 (what amounted to the family capital) 160 acres of pineland from one William H. Gregory. It was seven miles from the center of Miami and included a crude cabin-type dwelling and one half acre of cleared land planted in guavas. He bought it "sight unseen."

The plan was for Solomon and George to set out to prepare a home for Althea and the children, who would follow when that was accomplished. They stopped along the way to visit relatives in Maryland and, as it turned out, when they finally arrived at their destination they were turned back and refused entry. The yellow fever epidemic had hit Miami and a general quarantine was in effect. Stranded, they felt fortunate to be taken in by a clergyman friend who lived near Jupiter, where they remained for several months before being able to claim their new home in the summer of 1899.

George was thirteen, a strapping boy who proved capable of carrying a man's load from the moment they sailed into Biscayne Bay and south to Coconut Grove. They docked at Peacock Inn where they were warmly welcomed by Isabella and Charles Peacock. The Peacocks knew full well what it meant to pull up stakes and start over.

Back in 1875 Charles Peacock's reason for giving up a profitable wholesale meat business in foggy London town and taking off across the Atlantic ocean with his wife and three sons stemmed from the enthusiastic letters he was receiving from his brother. The latter was known as "Jolly Jack" when he homesteaded in Coconut Grove, and in fact the Grove was first known as Jack's Bight after the first Peacock to show his face in Florida. When he kept the House of Refuge for shipwrecked sailors at Miami Beach, it was said he stayed up all night reading adventure tales.

Charles and Isabella established the first inn, and it was there that their adored granddaughter, Eunice Isabella Peacock, was born. She was on hand to greet the newcomers that day. Far too young to remember the occasion, she was meeting her future husband, George Merrick, for the first time.

The first equipment needed by the Merricks was a mule and wagon. Once that was attended to, they set out for their new home.

Except for erecting the rough board and batten house and planting the guavas, the first owner failed to leave much of a mark during his brief stay.

The Merricks would.

From the first George assumed a partner's role in the new family enterprise. The work was back-breaking. Years later, his sister Ethel said that their father "almost gave up . . . it was George, fired with enthusiasm, who persuaded him to stay."

They had never seen guavas before, but that season there was a bumper crop and they gathered them up every day. George carried them to Coconut Grove to the home of Captain A. R. Simmons and his wife, the lady doctor Eleanor Galt Simmons, who practiced medicine traveling by pony and sailboat to those in need of treatment. She had given up her New York practice to follow her lawyer husband south for his health. The pair made tropical jellies and wines and shipped them north and abroad. They accepted all the Merrick pickings, and at the end of the guava season the earnings turned out to be two hundred dollars.

Cash money was hard to come by and for a while the Merricks called their home *Guavonia* in gratitude, meanwhile planting vegetables. Later they would put out oranges, and the new citrus fruit called grapefruit that was earning a reputation.

Solomon Merrick preached at Union Chapel, sometimes walking the distance to Coconut Grove. George took care of the hauling of materials from town, helped with the planting and, when the vegetables came in, played the role of family salesman, driving the mule cart door to door. That included the back door of the elegant Royal Palm, Henry Flagler's Victorian hotel at the mouth of the Miami River.

That first year George also took cabbages and potatoes regularly to the P & O dock, the only dock between Jacksonville and Key West, for shipment to Nassau and Cuba via Flagler's steamers.

It was a three hour trip to Miami along an old community trail, and one night as he was returning with a load of lumber for an addition to the cabin, the wagon broke down.

Much later he described it: "There I was, a timid kid, alone in the pitch black woods, peopled in my excited mind with panthers, wild cats and all kinds of ferocious animals thirsting for my blood."

The panthers were there all right. A pistol was considered a handy tool for a trip to town.

George unloaded the lumber from the wagon and set to work attempting to repair a broken coupling pole.

"In those days no one else would pass in a whole night on that road and sometimes not for days," he wrote.

"I had just reached the breaking point of my spirit when way off down the trail through the trees I saw a lantern bobbing about. I knew it was my father, after sixteen hours hard work, walking the seven miles to find out what the trouble was with me. I'll always remember the great throb of happy relief and deep affection I experienced that night."

Later, Merrick would name that trail Coral Way.

Early in January 1900 the long desired reunion of the Solomon Merrick family took place in Lemon City in a driving rain at midnight. Four exhausted children and one tired mother were met by husband and son but let Althea, herself, describe it:

"I had left my family in Pittsburgh a few days before with the assurance that I would stick it out in the unknown land of Florida for five years without going home but I felt a sinking of the heart. For three quarters of a mile we walked through a wood to the hotel in the rain, Mr. Merrick and George, who had met me carrying the youngest of the children.

"There was only one room for the seven of us and we were obliged to piece out the bed with chairs in order to get a fitful rest."

One of the first obstacles to peace of mind proved to be snakes and rats gaining access to the rafters and Althea solved the problem by lining the ceilings and walls with unbleached muslin.

She proved to be a master of improvisation. In three years' time, after her husband and sons built up a profitable produce business, she was ready with plans for a handsome rock home for her brood, increased in 1903 by the arrival of a third son, Richard. They called the home Coral Gables.

Althea gave painting lessons to all her children, but Richard would be the one to make it his life work. When he was a small boy, he informed his mother he wanted to stay home from school and paint "because the light was right." She understood and agreed. His works have been shown in prestigious galleries from the Museum of Modern Art in New York City to the Seattle Museum and the Corcoran in Washington, D. C. and are part of the permanent collections of the Library of Congress and the Palace of Fine Arts in Cuba.

George Merrick did not paint. He chose to paint his pictures with words and later go beyond words to create a physical world, but the brothers shared the same environment. There were always high quality art magazines and literature as well as music (by 1906 they had a piano) as daily fare, all provided in what was considered a backwoods.

The late Richard Merrick on the occasion of a retrospective show arranged to honor him on his eightieth birthday in 1983, explained how it was with him and art.

"I was, at an early age, well drenched . . . in the love of Whistler, Haden and Rembrandt, and the need to carry on tradition."

He was referring to his instruction at the Art Students League in New York, which he entered at the age of sixteen, but he might well have been referring to his home environment.

Charles, the third brother, worked in the groves and assisted in the shipping which eventually made the Merricks one of the largest producers in the state. Charles "got a hankering for the trowel" after having fallen under the influence of stonemasons imported to work on both the Gables and the new Plymouth Church. One in particular, a Spaniard named Felix Rabón "taught him the trade." The results of his work are everywhere and are included in the University of Miami area.

As the business prospered, Solomon Merrick turned his attention to his firstborn and decided a year at Rollins College would better prepare George for Law School at Columbia University. He had come to the decision that the Law would round out this gifted son's education.

While at Law School George stayed in Haworth, New Jersey at the home of his uncle, Denman Fink, a recognized artist. He wasn't too much older than George and they became fast friends. It was a happy time.

George wrote poetry. A short story, *The Sponger's Delilah*, took first prize in a contest and was published in a New York newspaper. He was on top of the world.

Then his father became ill and he was called home to look after the groves. Before the death of his father in 1911 a partnership was formed, S. G. Merrick and Son. They had been partners from the beginning.

Later George Merrick wrote: "After everyone was asleep my father was still up, planning and working here in this new and wonderful country . . . I was inspired by his courage and fortitude and perseverance in the sowing and caring for material, spiritual and intellectual plantings."

Vamp 'til Ready
1911-1921

THE death of his father ended the dream of becoming a writer for George Merrick. On his return from New York, he plunged wholeheartedly into the work of advancing the Merrick Plantation, the name given the groves when increased shipping business demanded printed statements.

It was a time of stability for his adopted land, with the financial panic of 1907 in the past and the present wrapped up in a celebration for Miami's fifteenth anniversary.

The first Mayor, John B. Reilly, declared: "There is perhaps nothing in the way of municipal improvements that Miami needs except the extension of paving sidewalks and sewers to the suburban areas."

J. W. Ewan, the Duke of Dade, given the name in the Florida Legislature, spoke at the celebration with a more imaginative turn of phrase, quoting Virgil: "As events which I myself saw and in which I was myself a chief participator . . ."

The automobile was appearing on streets, aviator Howard Gill flew his Wright biplane over the Miami skies to mark the birthday and, all in all, things looked mighty good.

George Merrick looked around and immediately became engulfed in it all.

In 1914 he was appointed to the Dade County Commission, a seat that provided ample opportunity for viewing the full impact of what lack of city planning could do. He began to buy real estate. In a few more years he had doubled the Merrick land holdings to 1200 acres and bought out his mother's interest although the money "came from the same pot" always.

Meanwhile, the tiny little girl, Eunice Peacock, had grown up and gone north to a school in Trenton, N. J. It was selected by Flora McFarlane, a teacher who lived in nearby Rocky Hill but who had homesteaded in Coconut Grove and had a strong hand in community developments.

Eunice, in her 90's, recalls clearly a conversation just before leaving for home after finishing school. She had been dating Princeton college boys and when the subject of available young men in Miami came up, Miss McFarlane suggested George Merrick as a candidate. "He's the last one I'd date," Eunice told her.

Eunice today has the same tinkly laugh she's always had.

"So I came right home and married him. We kind of clicked right off."

In a way they were made for each other. They shared the wilderness world, yet were exposed to the world of people of intellect and accomplishment of the times. To this day, Eunice keeps an autographed photograph of the actor Joseph Jefferson, an early visitor to Peacock Inn, on a side table.

The erudite Duke of Dade was her best friend when she was growing up. He lived in the Annex of Peacock Inn and formed the habit of reading to the child Eunice, filling her with poetry and the classics. They kept up a correspondence when she went away to school and he saved her letters.

In one dated October 1910 she refers to two instances of individuals recently married and asks the same question: "I wonder what she saw in *him*?" Of one she declares: "I would just as soon marry a scarecrow or a bean pole dressed up."

Eunice was noted for her independence and says today, "We were not brought up to be babies." As a child riding her bicycle down what is now McFarlane Road, she hit a palm tree— hard. There were injuries which she carefully kept hidden because "I was afraid they'd take my bicycle away."

Automobile rides to town on Saturday nights in George Merrick's "big Hudson" were part of the wooing process when they began to "date." So were dances at the Royal Palm Hotel. And in 1916 they were married.

Their honeymoon was a motor tour of Florida. They dropped in on friends in Orlando and other spots along the way as they drove north, stopping just south of Jacksonville.

George wrote a poem entitled *Moonlight in Old St. Augustine* which showed which way his mind was working and was an indication of things to be. Phrases which later would be put into action included "By pitted walls of ancient rose" and "Alad-

*Miss Eunice Isabella Peacock
of Coconut Grove.*

din-built, Alhambra-towered Inn." "Granada's wealth" entered into it as well.

The bridegroom built a honeymoon house near the Merrick family house which they called Poinciana Place, although it was always referred to in the family as The Bride's House.

Eunice remembers her mother's only question: "My goodness, won't you be lonely way out there?" Mrs. Alfred Peacock, born Lillian Frow, was not privy to her new son-in-law's hopes and dreams at the time, but her daughter says today, as she did then: "I've never been lonely in my life."

Instead, she was swept up into a quickening of her thirty-year-old husband's emerging dream of creating a shining city. Together they dug up Spanish names for streets not yet laid out, using for inspiration the sketches written by Washington Irving under the title *The Alhambra.* It was a game, but a game with serious intentions.

George began developing small sub-divisions in various parts of Miami, learning the ropes and making money at the same time. There was a lot going on and he was not one to live in a vacuum.

Carl G. Fisher had joined John Collins in helping him build a bridge to Miami Beach, which was incorporated in 1915 and as early as February 1913 developers were using the services of auctioneer Edward E. (Doc) Dammers to hawk land on both sides of Biscayne Bay. His showmanlike methods featured parachute exhibitions and balloon ascensions while giving away gifts of china and cutlery.

Hotels like the McAllister were being built, and for grandeur there was Villa Vizcaya, the James Deering extraordinary estate. It was finished the year Eunice and George were married.

All this entered into Merrick's vision and he was learning all the time what he wanted and did not want in the development of his city.

He began by inviting a trio of men of exceptional ability to share his dream and be in on the plans, selecting his uncle, Denman Fink, to provide the design for entrances and plazas. The latter described them as standing "constantly with a wide open-armed welcome to the passerby."

A Chicago landscape architect, Frank M. Button, who had been brought to Miami by Charles Deering, was put to work in 1921 on a horticultural plan. He spoke of "broad vistas . . . plazas and rest spots" and predicted that the individual walking in the planned city would pass "veritable bowers laden with delectable fruit."

H. George Fink, Merrick's cousin, would eventually design many early homes, as would Walter De Garmo, but Phineas E. Paist, a distinguished Philadelphia architect who worked on Vizcaya as well as the Willard Hotel in Washington, was in charge of the overall architectual scheme.

Solomon Merrick instigated the notion of selling tracts of land to retired ministers and professors in order to create a small colony of intellectuals and had actually sold a few to individuals who had built rock houses on what became Coral Way.

George's plans, when unveiled, went way beyond. They called for homesites for as many as ten thousand people living on five thousand acres in a "master suburb" with strict regulations for a community where the quality of life included overall architectural outlines and beauty was obligatory. These three planners all understood the desire for Spanish-Moorish design. Denman Fink explained it:

"We have taken for our motif such grand old Spanish cities as Cordova, Salamanca, Toledo and lovely old Seville. . . ."

A private celebration for Eunice and George Merrick in the form of an airplane trip to Nassau after the sale of the first lots in Coral Gables.

Always the plan included a grand hotel with a tower and a college graced with a tower. Those were particular Merrick specifications.

World War I was not a time for grandness, but it proved a time for dreaming and planning ahead.

When the war ended on November 11, 1918, Miami awakened to the sound of whistles and shouts of joy. The *Miami Daily Metropolis* and the *Herald* ran off extra editions, a victory parade brought blacks and whites together. It was a time for jubilation and it would not stop for quite a while.

The dreamer in George Merrick was alive and well. In 1920 he had a volume of poetry published in Boston. Called *Songs of the Wind on a Southern Shore*, it was illustrated by Denman Fink. In a poem, *When the Groves Begin to Bear*, he expressed sorrow that his father had not lived to see the beginnings of his success.

What would he have thought of what was to come?

Solomon most certainly would have cheered the fact that in 1918 the Plantation had shipped 107 carloads of citrus, ran two irrigating plants, and employed an overall average of fifty men who were helping develop nurseries.

That was the year Merrick was giving out the glad word that he planned to turn the plantation into that "master suburb." But it was not until July 1921 that he actually started clearing the land to make the first two streets, Coral Way and Granada Boulevard, and created Ponce de Leon Plaza.

On November fourteenth of that year Merrick took out a huge double page newspaper advertisement in which he declared that the "building of Coral Gables was a wonderful monument to the achievement of worthwhile perseverance in the creation of beauty and the coming true of dreams."

He sent buses into Miami to bring prospective buyers and on November twenty-eighth they came. Some said that it was mainly to be entertained by Doc Dammers.

What they thought about the Plaza sticking up in a wasteland known to them mostly as "the sticks" was not much. They thought it was bizarre most of them, not being equipped with the Merrick line of vision.

But on November twenty-ninth the first building lot was sold on their front lawn, and George and Eunice celebrated by taking an airplane trip to Nassau. They were off on more than an airplane ride. What lay ahead for them was a razzle dazzle ride on a roller coaster spelled b-o-o-m. Nothing would ever be the same again.

'What Great Plans
and Ideas ...'

L OOKING back on it, Eunice Merrick will tell you that "it all happened so quickly when George was building Coral Gables." The beginning was not nearly quick enough to suit her husband.

The trouble was that Miami bankers, with their eyes turned to the practical realization of profits on investments, simply did not see eye to eye with Merrick or his ideas for a planned city. Who in the world would want to live in a place where you were told how to build your house and what color to paint it? It was positively un-American. Why bother, when all around subdivisions were springing up closer to the center of town?

On the other hand, Merrick felt he was being practical since he was planning to build homes in various price ranges for a broad spectrum of society. He had been building homes in a number of subdivisions and felt qualified to judge what would sell.

He confessed later that going hat in hand to obtain financial assistance had been humiliating, and that once he had contemplated giving up on the idea. "They called me a visionary and sometimes they were not so complimentary," he said.

At that important moment of hesitation, a friend from his days at Rollins College re-entered his life.

Charles F. Baldwin, always known as Jack Baldwin, came to Miami after service in World War I because his family had moved here from Central Florida. He had served in the Twenty-eighth Infantry Division, had newspaper experience before the war, and went to work for the *Metropolis*. The meeting was providential for George because Baldwin also had links with an insurance company, the Jefferson Standard.

When Merrick explained his need for funds with which to proceed, Baldwin suggested they try the insurance people. The result was the underwriting of the first one hundred homes in Coral Gables. That was the beginning of George Merrick's private boom.

Baldwin's son, C. Jackson Baldwin, also known as Jack, recalls the family story of Merrick urging the Baldwins to move at once to Coral Gables. Mrs. Baldwin was aghast. She was not about to move "way out there" where there weren't even telephones. "I'll get you one and it will be the first installed," Merrick promised. The number was Evergreen One, but when it was offered to Jack, he said, "Your mother should have it. We'll take the second." Baldwin would remain with Merrick throughout his operation, serving as treasurer.

It seemed that all at once there was no lack of money. Eventually, trips to New York for Eunice and George meant a whole floor at the Biltmore, designer dresses, and doors to bankers and financiers held invitingly open. George began to build a larger house for Eunice which she first refused to inspect because she preferred Poinciana Place, but the day came when she moved in gracefully and without protest.

Marjory Stoneman Douglas remembers being invited to write early material relating to Coral Gables "for a couple of hundred dollars," but within no time at all New York writer Rex Beach was being paid $25,000 for the same service. The days of going hat in hand to Miami bankers and being turned down, often with unfriendly laughter, were ended for George Merrick. "He was really spending money," Mrs. Douglas recalls.

T. H. Weigall, the British journalist who joined the Coral Gables Corporation as a publicity writer, found out that "he retained his control with an iron hand. Nothing could be done without his approval; nothing could be held back when once he had ordered that it should go forward. His will was law, absolute and immutable but he kept his head. Working far into the night he appeared in public less and less so that he became a strange and mysterious power. . . ."

By the time he reached the age of thirty-seven, Merrick was by way of becoming a legend. Mrs. Douglas said it this way: "He remained aloof . . . the Great Man."

By 1925 he had spent one hundred million dollars on improvements for his city and five million went for publicizing it.

Front man William Jennings Bryan uses the Coral Gables trolley car as a platform to preach the gospel of Coral Gables.

Dr. Frank Crane, hired to write advance blurbs for the Miami Biltmore, in the summer of 1925 called it "the last word in the history of civilization." He declared: "At this place with all its inducements to rest and leisure what great plans and ideas may be born in the minds of leaders who gather here in the days to come?"

In the same elaborate brochure which contained arresting illustrations by Chester B. Price, Crane said: "This Hotel and Country Club will attract the right kind of people to the land. People with money are no better than people without it. But there is no question that they do more good to the country they live in. They employ labor and increase the value of property and the Miami Biltmore Country Club by attracting this kind of people draws the South to the attention of the moneyed men of the country."

Flushed with success, George Merrick remarked: "Beauty can be made to pay." At the same time he also turned down a fortune for a large part of his holdings with the words, "This is more money than Mrs. Merrick and I shall ever need but we are here for a different purpose." Steadfastly, he continued marching forward to paint the ordained picture he carried in his head.

He organized the Coral Gables Corporation to handle his business. That was quickly followed by the incorporation of

Coral Gables as a city on April 27, 1925. It was announced then that the City would be governed by a five member Commission which included Merrick, his friend Baldwin, Telfair Knight, F. W. Webster, and the indefatigable Doc Dammers. He became the first Mayor of Coral Gables on May first, at the first meeting of the Commission.

The idea of establishing a university began to gain ground in Miami, and Merrick immediately did everything in his power to locate it in Coral Gables.

Judge W. E. Walsh had obtained a charter for the proposed University of Miami and the new regents were considering land sites offered by real estate developers. George Merrick, with Eunice by his side, drove around the Gables trying to pick out the most appropriate site for the college he envisioned.

Under consideration at one point had been the site of the Biltmore. Next Coral Way and Red Road was considered, but Merrick finally decided to give 160 acres at what is the present location of the University of Miami. This was the exact amount of land his father started out with in 1899.

Lots of people stood in line offering to sell land to the budding institution. Merrick was the only one to offer the gift of land. He tacked on an offer of five million dollars to launch an endowment fund and encourage others to do the same. Merrick's offer was the one accepted. He set about having plans drawn for the new university, in the Mediterranean style, of course, and with a tower.

Things were moving according to plan, all neat and tidy and pushing toward the big splash of opening the Biltmore, but there were also other preoccupations.

There was that business of the Biscayne Bay section of Coral Gables with specifications for a beach measuring six and a half miles on which a casino, a yacht club, and another hotel with one thousand rooms would rise at Cocoplum, renamed Tahiti Beach. Incidentally, it should be noted that it was a period when the word casino did not necessarily connote gambling. Instead, it indicated a resort gathering place. This applied to the projected development as well as the Venetian Pool and Hardie's Casino at Miami Beach.

Rex Beach wrote: "Ten years of hard work, a hundred millions of hard money is what George Merrick plans to spend be-

Men among the Mangrove: left to right, Charles Flynn, George Merrick, Roy Jackson, and John Bowman, all bent on selecting the site for that one thousand room hotel and casino at Cocoplum on Biscayne Bay.

fore he rests. Who can envisage what ten years will bring to that wonderland of Ponce de Leon's? . . . "

As the Biltmore neared completion Merrick decided to have a second office in the Tower.

Perhaps,— who knew?— he might be able to write poetry in snatched moments.

An emissary of Queen Marie of Rumania was forced to cool his heels one day in the outer office of the developer because, a secretary explained, he "could not be disturbed because he was busy writing poetry."

Light Up the Sky

THEY lit up the Giralda Tower for the first time and celebrated the official opening of the Miami Biltmore with a running series of shining events, beginning with the banquet at the Country Club for a select two hundred "dignitaries" on January 14, 1926.

Photographs of Merrick and Bowman appeared on the cover of an oversized handsome souvenir menu which offered pheasant and sea trout among other delicacies and, oh yes, a few well chosen words from the pen of Dr. Frank Crane.

His prediction was that "many people may come and go but this structure will remain a thing of lasting beauty."

Bowman, rising to speak at the banquet, declared: "Another vision has become a reality and we have, through brain, brawn and muscle, a 1950 hotel model built like a modern Biltmore noted for beauty, utility and endurance."

Merrick remembered that "only twenty years ago . . . my father and myself were clearing little vegetable patches around it. . . . Even eight years ago I was growing tomatoes on the very ground on which this great hotel is built."

People were streaming in from northern cities on special trains marked "Miami Biltmore Specials," and the trip from New York was establishing a new record of thirty-six hours, twenty-three minutes.

The Formal Opening Inspection of the hotel and club and the Formal Dinner Dance and Fashion Show were set for the fifteenth of January. Those in charge "deeply regretted" the fact that only fifteen hundred guests could be accommodated for the evening and that thirty-five hundred had to be turned away for that event.

In order to appease those who could not dine and dance at the opening, there was scheduled the following week daily showings of the lavish fashion show, which featured two hundred and fifty

Story Motor Mart Will
Rise on Site of Indian Fort

COURT ALMOST
IDLE WITH LONE

Demand for Cooks in Miami
Said to Far Exceed Supply

They came from far and wide to be present at the formal opening dinner dance of the Miami Biltmore Hotel.

thousand dollars worth of feminine finery. Fifteen of Manhattan's most in-demand models, called "manikins," were transported along with the clothes, measured to provide a total of three hundred and fifty outfits.

Prunella Wood, who made her mark as a syndicated fashion writer, recalled it this way: "Lovely gowns and gorgeous furs, heavenly scents and beautiful jewels." She observed that "satin was the pet fabric, mostly white or in glowing gem tones. Skirts were long and slim, topped by elaborate bodices contrived with bead embroidery or sheer lace."

The men stuck to the traditional black and white; many wore tails. Prunella had a good word to say for them too.

"I remember only handsome men," she said, "and ever so many of them."

The "inspection" of the hotel, posted by the management as a feature of the opening festivities, was warranted. There were four hundred guest rooms and suites. Each had a private bath and at the ready was a staff of a thousand to care for guests.

One of the three ballrooms was large enough to permit "five hundred fox-trotting couples."

Do you suppose they counted couples on the floor the night of January fifteenth? No matter, there was room for dancing all over the place, both indoors and outdoors. Paul Whiteman and two other orchestras played, the latter recruited from the Westchester Biltmore along with the head chef, a fellow named Durand with his large staff. Lanterns flickered and champagne corks popped, evidence that the Riviera of America was being properly launched "under the sheltering palms."

Prohibition was ostensibly in effect but one observer of the scene during the boomtime maneuvers declared that "there must have been more alcohol per head consumed in Florida than in any other country in the world."

Too bad about the lady who upset the gondola, complete with gondolier, imported from Italy to grace the swimming pool. At the height of the festivities, overcome by excitement, she plunged into the swimming pool, causing the handsome Italian to fall into the drink along with her.

It is rumored that the Tower light blinked once. Suffice it to say the combined openings proved breathtaking enough for all concerned. The *Miami Daily News* called the formal opening "such splendor as has been rarely seen," while the *New York Times* stuck to statistics by pointing out that Coral Gables was now "a city of ten thousand acres covering sixteen square miles with population of more than seventy five hundred."

The gondolier, one of several imported to brighten the scene, spent the remainder of the highly successful season ferrying guests on the canals where he succeeded in avoiding being dunked.

One of the town's favorite stories occurred when a prominent matron, Mrs. Harry (Grace) Hector experienced a similar fate as that of the gondolier's and certainly not of her doing.

It was during a dramatic moment in a Bobby Jones play in one of the exciting golf tournaments that dotted the greens at the Biltmore, and Mrs. Hector was one of many crowding a small bridge over the canal in order to catch a better view. The bridge began to give way under the weight of the occupants, and while others scurried to safety, Mrs. Hector was caught in the middle. As the story was stated she "went down with the bridge."

Both gondola and gondolier
were imported to ride the
canals from the Biltmore to
Biscayne Bay on romantic
tours for hotel guests.

Her daughter Emily Maxted, remembers that "she sank in her white suit and as she rose she said, 'My, that was refreshing.'" A son, lawyer Louis J. Hector, reports her picture was taken by an alert photographer covering the golf match, and that it appeared in *Time Magazine*. Another son, Robert C. Hector, longtime State legislator, recalls that the Biltmore picked up the dry cleaning bill for his mother.

The Biltmore collected its share of headlines in the weeks following the opening, as morning horseback rides competed for attention in a crowded schedule of events. The *Miami Riviera* declared that "Coral Gables had achieved permanent fame as a resort of superior quality and character" and proceeded to print a roll of honor of those who showed up. On the list were Otto Kahn; Bernard Baruch; Albert Lasker; Feodor Chaliapin; Mary Garden and the entire cast of the Chicago Grand Opera Company, including Giovanni Martinelli.

Add Ida M. Tarbell; and, from the film world, Jesse L. Lasky, Adolph Zukor, Thomas Meighan, and Lila Lee; throw in important sports figures Gene Tunney, Tex Rickard, and Gene

Bobby Jones, far left, and his fans.

Sarazen; and you have a fair idea of who was walking the fairways or riding the gondolas in the winter of 1926. Assuredly, the Biltmore was living up to its press agentry and attracting visitors from all over the world.

The affable James J. Walker, who left the State Senate to beat out John F. Hylan for Mayor of New York, a role he played to the hilt, appeared on the scene. A "mayoral walking tour" was arranged by Doc Dammers. Wearing a tweed cap and suit with a vest, Jimmy had little trouble keeping up with the "Doc" (the nickname came from having been a pharmacist, it was said) as they travelled about, followed by a cameraman lugging heavy equipment.

One of the highlights of Walker's visit was the arrival of the cruiser *Cuba*, the flagship of the Cuban Navy, to transport him to Havana for an official visit. Nothing would do but that Doc Dammers go along as Mayor of Coral Gables and, as usual, he traveled with a retinue of sorts. His automobile was adorned with a coronet that lit up so that his visibility was undoubted. His companions on the trip to Cuba were Charles Flynn, who

Guests at the Biltmore off for a morning canter.

had "personally supervised" the building of the Miami Biltmore, Police Chief M. P. Lehman of Coral Gables, and publicity man Weigall.

A special delegation was accompanying the flagship on its mission, so it was decided the Mayors & Co. would board the flagship as a courtesy gesture before the delegation was transported to an elaborate luncheon at the Miami Biltmore Country Club. Also arranged was a police escort to the hotel with officers from both Miami and Miami Beach joining the Coral Gables force to present a united welcome front bordering on a parade.

The weather did not cooperate at the moment for boarding the Cuban vessel, and the frustrated members of the party aboard the *Marionette* were thoroughly drenched and tossed about. All they could manage two miles out where the *Cuba* lay at anchor was to wave a feeble white handkerchief (that would be Doc) and retreat "half stunned and half drowned," as Weigall described it.

They made up for it with the reception committee ashore where an orchestra remained on the alert. As the visitors from Cuba came ashore, the music broke out: the "Cuban National Anthem" first, of course, then "The Sidewalks of New York" for Jimmy Walker.

What with one thing or another the party sat down to luncheon at exactly five P.M. It went on until dark so that there was scarcely time to change for the formal dinner, but change they all did, and that night the rafters rang to toasts raised to the United States of America and the Cuban Republic.

Breezes stirred the palm trees in which lights twinkled along with the stars in the heavens and, from time to time, eyes turned to the light in the Tower which seemed to encompass the scene in a most friendly fashion.

It was close to dawn when the party raced toward the Royal Palm docks and prepared to board a waiting launch to carry them to the flagship waiting to transport them all to Havana. That is quite another story, but rest assured Doc Dammers had in mind selling some Coral Gables real estate when they reached the Sevilla Biltmore in Havana.

There a new round of gayety, with the Cuban government playing host, went on for days, and where the debonair Jimmy Walker went on making friends and influencing people while enjoying horse racing, jai alai, and endless listening to "The Sidewalks of New York," all of which he took in graceful stride. It was a heyday for Hizzoner as well as the Biltmore. The Seabury investigation citing corruption in government was a half dozen years in the future, along with his hasty resignation and flight to Europe until things cooled down.

Goodbye to the Roaring Twenties

THERE are three words that have come to describe all of it: The Boom, the Blow, and the Bust.

Historian Charlton W. Tebeau puts it into perspective when he says: "The 1926 blow did not kill the boom but it certainly buried it in devastating fashion."

We have been hearing about the boom, and most of us know that the blow means the roaring September hurricane, but the bust had been coming on months before the breathtaking opening of the Miami Biltmore.

The crash of 1929 which caused men to jump out of windows in New York's financial district began in Miami three years earlier.

Experts figure that the Florida boom began in the Spring of 1923 when building periods from April through July totalled one and a half million dollars a month. Then, in one month—August 1924—building rose to four million dollars, and the peak was reached in the Fall of 1925 when the building permits for the Miami area reached $15,787,539. That was probably the start of the national depression.

A series of events put an end to the joyride of the Florida boom. It started as far back as August 1925 when the Florida East Coast Railroad found it necessary to call a temporary freight embargo in order to repair tracks that had been taking a beating in the rush of people and materials to South Florida. N.B.T. Roney always said it hurt him more than the hurricane.

Some developers surreptitiously brought in building materials in refrigerated cars intended for food, but most turned to the sea to transport their supplies. Miami waters became a forest of masts as everything floatable was pressed into service.

In dramatic fashion a few days before the opening of the Biltmore, the barkentine *Prins Valdemar* went aground. She was an old Danish Naval training ship rigged up as a floating hotel, and it happened at the entrance to the turning basin as she was being towed to Miami Beach to open up for the season. There she stayed for close to a month blocking the entire harbor entrance and driving developers wild.

The Biltmore remained relatively unaffected and continued to fulfill its destiny as a center for the rich and great for the next eight months. Then came the hurricane of September eighteenth. It was the kiss of death for extended high living and elegance for some time to come. The morning of that very day Merrick had mailed out 2000 letters announcing his winter season.

The general population was generally oblivious to the storm warnings posted. It was only veterans of the subtropics who made preparations for the hurricane which hit shortly after midnight. It raged throughout the black night, the first hurricane of any account since 1906 when the "extension workers" on Flagler's railroad to Key West had been caught, many facing death. When it was over, so was the boom.

At the Biltmore, windows were blown out during fierce winds. Draperies, rugs, and furnishings all took a beating—but Bowman had been right about the Biltmore "enduring." It stood through winds clocked at 128 miles an hour before the last wind gauge blew away and came through far better than most, thanks to the strict building code Merrick had provided. About two thousand people found assistance one way or another behind its massive front doors during the storm and in it's shocking aftermath.

The damage throughout the general area was awesome, hurricanes not having figured in most builder's specifications. But in Coral Gables Frank Button, the landscape artist, had a crew out in a matter of days restoring trees and bushes to their original positions.

The answer to any unfavorable notice had always been for Florida to pour out more words of praise for the region. Such had been the case the month before the hurricane struck when a delegation of big wheels including Governor John W. Martin, George Merrick, and Carl Fisher went to New York and put on a

The vessel Rose Mahoney was swept ashore by the '26 hurricane. A piece of her mast went into a memorial flagpole for John McEntee Bowman.

"Truth About Florida" banquet at the Waldorf Astoria, inviting the nation's press in order to "set the record straight."

When the September storm hit, out-of-town papers wrote obituaries for South Florida. The known dead reached one hundred and thirteen in Dade County. A good many went to their graves unidentified. A typical headline read: *South Florida Wiped Out in Storm.*

The story in the Merrick family was that when George was a boy and had a toothache, he didn't complain. Instead, he went outdoors and threw rocks against the barn. Now he simply marched ahead attempting to deal with the stream of people departing from Florida, leaving behind a trail of unpaid mortgages. Once again bankers were not proving that friendly.

In the middle of it all the man in charge of Merrick's fishing camp on the Keys absconded with the profits.

In spite of everything George Merrick had no intention of giving up. In the Fall of 1927 he and Eunice were in New York, stopping at the Biltmore as usual. They were there for the express purpose of drumming up financial support, and it wasn't going his way.

Richard Merrick was studying painting at the Art Students League and driving a cab, and one of the light spots of the trip for Eunice was being returned to the Biltmore by Richard one day and saying to the taxi driver in the presence of the doorman, "I'll see you at dinner."

It was one of only a few light spots.

A letter dated October twenty-eighth from Althea Merrick to her daughter-in-law tells much:

"My dear little Eunice: I just received a little letter from George. He said some very nice things about you. I know just how perplexed and worried he is and also just how hard it all is for you. But Eunice I just want to tell you how much your patience and love to my big boy binds you closer to me. . . . Much love, Mother Merrick."

In the early 1920s Althea had remodeled the family home, adding a garage and servants quarters. Now she was on the eve of having to make another change and would be ready to face it when the time came. She would add five bathrooms and take in paying guests, calling the old home place Merrick Manor. Ethel Merrick thought up the name.

When the crash was felt by the country as a whole, Coral Gables had two thousand residences and not just for the rich. Merrick had also provided modest homes. His check book failed to balance but he left in place a "balanced city," which was his goal all the time. There was a new City Hall, there were business and industrial sections, wide avenues, fountains, and beautiful homes. Beauty remained and didn't go away. Neither did George Merrick. He began to face his debtors.

A builder to whom Merrick owed money had always admired the "partner desk" at which Solomon Merrick and his son had faced each other during the early days of the Coral Gables Plantation while they worked on shipment orders for the groves. The builder was given the desk in part payment for what was owed him. You can see it today in the Coral Gables House, now a museum created in the old Merrick home. It was donated by the builder.

The Biltmore continued to stay open with dinner dances, golf tournaments, and aquatic events. It was the aquatic show at

They came by the thousands on Sunday afternoon to view the lavish aquatic shows staged by Alexander Ott.

the Biltmore that drew the crowds, as many as three thousand on a Sunday afternoon.

We have this on no less an authority than Jackie Ott, the boy wonder who starred in his father Alexander Ott's water show and lived on the sixth floor of the Biltmore for thirteen years.

You've heard of *Eloise at the Plaza*? Now consider Jackie Ott at the Biltmore.

In between diving from the eighty-five foot pedestal of "the largest swimming pool in the world," Jackie's big thing was playing marbles "with the rich kids." He recalls with understandable satisfaction that he managed to "win all their marbles." Sometimes when he balked at making the high leap into the pool, his father would "pay him off in marbles." He remembers every marble with affection. "Some were so beautiful you could've made them into rings."

Jackie's best friends in the adult world were swimmers: Pete Desjardins, Stubby Kruger, and Johnny Weissmuller, who broke the world record at the Biltmore pool. His tree-swinging days in Tarzan films lay ahead.

*Three champions: Johnny
Weissmuller, Jackie Ott, and
Pete Desjardins.*

Jackie says the young Weissmuller was "inclined to be a hell-raiser" back in those days. "He only drank milk but the night he was found running naked down the corridors and the time he turned in the fire alarm just for the hell of it, the manager wanted to kick him out."

One day Swedish swimming star Arne Borg (who did drink booze and smoked cigars as well) decided to enter a race in order to obtain the prize. It was a case of choice alcohol but he didn't want to get carried away and break his record with too high a margin.

"If I go too fast wave me down with a towel," he instructed Weissmuller. Johnny did as he was told but Arne mistook the signal and broke the record by more than he wanted which made him furious. He was saving it for a better occasion.

It was Weissmuller who drove Jackie Ott over to the West Flagler Dog Track the night Jackie won the popularity contest. The prize was an airplane. It was sold later to R. S. Evans, the used car dealer. Jackie said, "It wasn't that I was so popular. It was that my dad was such a promoter."

All through the depression the Aquatic Show made money for the Biltmore. Everybody got excited when "Alligator Jack" Cop-

Fly the flags and beat the drums. This March 3, 1929 photograph shows how the Miami Biltmore was dealing with the depression. This was a bathing beauty contest won by Marjorie Kohn of New York City.

pinger wrestled the "live Everglades Amphibians." Whole families attended the shows and those without children went tea dancing to Carlos Molina's orchestra afterwards.

"The dining room was like a morgue sometimes," Jackie said "My father was the only one writing figures in black ink."

Emmett Kelly, the clown; Sonja Henie, the ice skating film queen—Jackie knew them all, and for that matter he played in a motion picture called *Born Rich* starring Claire Windsor, Bebe Daniels, and Bert Lytell.

Was that fun?

"Not really. The most fun was sweeping out the studios with the big broom whenever they'd let me."

What was really fun was a dark secret. Jackie and a small bunch of small boys had a "secret clubhouse" clear up at the top of the Tower. The boys lucky enough to be members stole up to the final ladder, then swung over and dropped themselves into the copper dome. There they would "sit down and shoot the breeze." They kept a stock of confetti and tin horns left over from New Year's Eve parties for their own private celebration. Jackie's mother, Grace, kept scrapbooks of her son's doings and calculated that he had appeared in thirty-two newsreels. Nobody ever got a photograph of the intrepid climbers who made the dome of the Biltmore Tower their childhood reserve.

Jack Ott today, after Navy service as a flyer and twenty-eight years of managing Dade County swimming pools, runs a highly profitable boat yard which he named "Ott's Yachts."

In spite of valiant efforts, on April 13, 1929, Merrick's Coral Gables Corporation declared bankruptcy. After a first mortgage amounting to $1,800,000 was foreclosed, a friendly agreement by bondholders resulted in the formation of a new corporation. The Miami Biltmore would remain open, but not for long. The *New York Times* of July 1, 1930, delivered the bad news. Once again the Biltmore was in default.

They asked Merrick to resign from the City Commission of the city he had founded. It appeared members blamed him for the big blow and the bust but never thought to thank him for his efforts in connection with the boom.

George Merrick began planning with his brother Richard a motor trip that would take them on a tour of the USA with a dip into Mexico. He had in mind looking around at what had been happening to the rest of his country while he had been so absorbed in a night and day operation that had, all at once it seemed, come to an end. Carefully he plotted the trip on maps and waited for the right moment to take off.

On August sixth the two brothers set forth driving to Fort Myers as the first stop. George carried a little notebook in which he was prepared to write down every penny spent. The first entry was: "Gas, $4.00 and Breakfast, $1.00" The notebook, filled with figures written in heavy black pencil, is a road map of what the brothers did.

In Tia Juana the first entry is "Beer and Gambling, $10.00" and "Supper $1.00." That was on August seventeenth. The next day there was this entry: "Gambler Loss, $8.00." The fact that $2.00 was spent for an art magazine in San Francisco comes as no surprise. The pair really splurged in San Francisco, where they spent "$4.50 for Cleaning and Pressing, $8.00 for Sightseeing and $11.00 for Shows." That was between August twenty-fifth through twenty-seventh. Of course they took

On the keys: George Merrick, left, and his brother Richard.

the ferry to Sausalito and then drove up the California coast and into Oregon, Washington State, and Vancouver.

In all they were gone more than six weeks and drove home by way of Montana, Wyoming, Iowa, and Chicago, spelling each other at the wheel. In Chicago they succumbed once again to theatre and the costs were duly entered by George. Their last stop was Dublin, Georgia.

Some place along the way George decided to start all over again on the Keys where he owned the camp. As they drove along, he was observing a new type of traveler in the middle class range and he decided to plan something new. He would open a fishing lodge for these travelers and distinguish it not with elegance this time but with good taste and good food. What he was envisioning, his brother Richard always said, was an early motel and not just for fishermen.

Richard designed additions, a former chef from the Roney Plaza was enlisted, and people like the David Fairchilds found it to their liking. Merrick began to promote the Key Lime pie.

Would you believe it all blew away in the terrible hurricane that hit the Keys in 1935?

Name Dropping
Through the 1930s

BOWMAN looked around and came up with some new backers for the Biltmore, and among them was John J. Raskob, vice president of General Motors and chairman of the finance committee. Raskob listed himself in *Who's Who In America* as "capitalist."

He had been a staunch Republican; but in order to back Governor Alfred E. Smith of New York, he switched parties and was tapped as chairman of the Democratic National Committee. The Governor was a member of the group buying into the crippled Biltmore, and Raskob announced that the Tower would become the new Little White House.

Not so fast. There was Herbert Hoover waiting in the wings. Fate had tapped *him* for the presidency.

Al Smith made his bid for the highest office in the land and managed to sleep at the Biltmore on a brief visit, but the Biltmore Tower never became the Little White House.

The Governor of the Empire State also managed to play some golf, and one publicized match was set up with the King of Swat, Babe Ruth.

After one season Raskob and Smith bowed out and in rode Colonel Henry Latham Doherty, who had accumulated a vast fortune in Cities Service, a billion dollar holding company for public utilities and petroleum properties. The new one-man backer arrived not a moment too soon. Six weeks later John McEntee Bowman was dead. His death at Post Graduate Hospital in New York on October 28, 1931, was followed by a large funeral that began at his Biltmore Hotel, proceeded to the Central Presbyterian Church, and ended at Hillside Cemetery, Rutherford, N. J. The *New York Times* quoted the president of the American Hotel Association, who called it "a deep and irreparable loss" and spoke affectionately of the "helping hand of Jack Bowman."

The few alive who remember him from his Miami and Havana days speak of his sartorial style and impeccable manners. Loretta Sheehy, who came as a young girl from Waterbury, Conn. to serve as a secretary in Merrick's Coral Gables Corporation later becoming the city clerk, found him to be "gallant, fastidious, a professional to his fingertips."

Percy P. Steinhart, a banker who left Cuba for Venezuela and New York after Castro rose to power, is the grandson of Frank M. Steinhart, a colorful partner of Bowman's in Cuba. The elder Steinhart went there with Teddy Roosevelt's Rough Riders, was later appointed Consul General of the United States, and stayed on to form the partnership. The pair headed numerous important enterprises. Today, settled in Coral Gables and an active supporter of the museum, Percy Steinhart carries a small-boy memory of Bowman as a glamorous figure wearing white flannel trousers and a Panama hat and of being a kindly presence.

Bowman's passing from the scene did not go unobserved in Coral Gables. A flagpole was erected in his memory at the Biltmore and, in what seemed an appropriate gesture, the pole that flew Old Glory had begun life as part of the five-masted schooner *Rose Mahoney*, blown ashore in the '26 hurricane, the storm that sounded the death knell for the Biltmore and the rest of south Florida. A copper weather vane depicting two golfing figures topped off the flagpole. It had been designed by Bowman himself, as friends observed at the ceremony. Those baring their heads were three giant developers: Merrick, Roney, Fisher—and the most recent owner of the Biltmore, Henry L. Doherty.

In order to understand the impact of multi-millionaire Doherty's taking command of the troubled Biltmore finances, a reminder of the times is in order. President Hoover had seen the need for federal assistance and that year formed "The President's Organization on Unemployment Relief." Because the idea seemed foreign, Florida actually turned down federal assistance—but times were tough. Denman Fink, who had created all the beautiful entrances and arches in Coral Gables, figured out how to get his meals by making a deal with a downtown restaurant: all he could eat in exchange for his paintings.

Things would improve. Joseph E. Widener was able to get through the Florida Legislature the legalization of parimutuel betting for Hialeah racetrack. This provided impetus for the

*Colonel Henry L. Doherty
poured a fortune into the
Florida Year Round Clubs in
the 1930s and gave the
Biltmore a new lease on life.*

track to emerge as a star attraction in addition to earning much needed money for state coffers and creating a lure for visitors to the Biltmore.

Colonel Doherty was a one-man bona fide relief program, a forerunner of all the alphabet organizations that the New Deal would provide. The first thing he did was hire Carl Byoir, who had been present at the ground breaking of the hotel, to crank up his publicity machine. The word went out to light up empty rooms when night fell.

One of Byoir's attention-getters in a barrage of press releases was the suggestion that Colonel Doherty was "one of the three great Henrys," the others being Flagler and Plant, whose feats had been to open up the state of Florida with their railroads. In an effort to make the Biltmore more attractive for winter visitors, Doherty purchased the Roney Plaza at Miami Beach for ocean swimming and the Key Largo Anglers Club for fishermen. They were named the Florida Year Round Clubs.

It was Newt Roney who supplied the title, actually. He had been fighting to hold on to his hotel, had spent two hundred thousand dollars constructing a swimming pool and cabana area. In the year before selling out to Doherty, he spent an additional one hundred thousand in advertising on the national scene in magazines, radio, and newspapers. Using the term "year round" was a piece of wishful thinking in the period when 'the season' began around Christmas and ended after two months even in good times.

Doherty purchased fancy buses to tie all three places together. They were given the fancy name of Aerocars. A forerunner of the helicopter was called an Autogyro and was handy for vacationers in a hurry. A boat to Key Largo was given the name Sea Sled, which turned out to be a term used in Rex Beach's boomtime literature.

Charles G. (Bebe) Rebozo, who later became a close friend and confidant of President Richard Nixon, remembers driving an Aerocar for fifty cents an hour and "being glad to get it." He recalls that "five hundred lined up for the few jobs." Because of demonstrating skill and diligence on the job, Rebozo ended up as a steward down at Key Largo at the Anglers Club, where he was paid eighteen dollars a week.

Not everybody was hard up, of course. Take Howard Hughes. The eccentric millionaire injured his shoulder while visiting the Cascades Bar at the Biltmore and Dr. Arthur Weiland, who had been the first president of the Country Club, and who lived across the street, was called. Before the doctor could reach him, Hughes had sped off with a group of young ladies for his yacht berthed at Miami Beach at the Nautilus Hotel, leaving word that he'd see the doctor there. Dr. Weiland called his friend Dr. Tom Otto at Miami Beach and asked him to look in on Hughes, which he did, finding him "surrounded by girls." Dr. Tom treated him and sent a bill for fifty dollars, a sum of money Howard Hughes deemed was "too high." Dr. Tom sent back word that he would consider this "a charity case" and Hughes could "consider the bill paid." A check for fifty dollars was forthcoming in the return mail.

The Doherty purse strings were never tightly held. In no time at all, he was by way of becoming the benefactor for the town. Miami lawyer Thomas H. Wakefield remembers participating in a private performance of the Miami Drum and Bugle Corps for the colonel on the Biltmore terrace before setting forth to play in Philadelphia, New York, and Washington, D. C., where another private performance took place at the White House for President

The Colonel's lady Mrs. Henry L. Doherty, entertains movie star Deanna Durbin in the Tower suite of the Biltmore.

Hoover. Doherty underwrote the entire schoolboy operation sponsored by the Junior Chamber of Commerce.

When three thousand dollars was needed to stage the first annual New Year's Day football game between the University of Miami and Manhattan College, he gave the money for that. Later the name was changed from Palm Festival to Orange Festival and a tradition was born. It was a strike against the depression and would become a mammoth nationally-televised sports attraction which Sports Editor Edwin Pope recently declared: " . . . has done more than anything except sun and sand for South Florida tourism in the last half century."

Who was this saviour who appeared out of nowhere and increasingly was referred to as Colonel?

The title was honorary, but, as somebody said, it sort of "went with his trim beard." It was also said that the Colonel's lady, Grace, was partial to giving parties and the Biltmore provided a proper background for them. They increased in number and splendor as the Helen Lee Doherty Milk Fund Ball, named for her daughter, and the Aviation Ball were introduced to the Country Club calendar. One who attended them, Paula Baker, recalls taking lessons from her mother in how to dance while holding up a train.

You might say the Colonel served as a benefactor for members of the press as well. Out-of-town newspaper reporters could stay at the Biltmore for a dollar a night and this included free booze. They in turn reciprocated by adding the Miami Biltmore to their datelines. Publicity was the name of the game and Carl Byoir knew all the rules. Therefore, when an event of national and international importance occurred in Miami, there was no question as to where the correspondents would congregate. The Biltmore's lower floor was instantly turned into a working press area complete with Teletype.

It was a soft pleasant evening on February 13, 1933, when twenty thousand Miamians gathered at the Bandshell in Miami's Bayfront Park to greet the President-Elect of the United States, Franklin Delano Roosevelt. He had been relaxing on his friend Vincent Astor's yacht *Nourmahal* fishing in the Bahamas and was scheduled to make a short talk.

Mayor R. B. Gautier Sr. arrived with FDR in an open touring car from which he delivered the speech. That ended, he settled back in the car, first waving to his old friend Mayor Anton Cermak of Chicago who was seated in the grandstand, indicating he wanted him to join him. The rest is history: "a sound like firecrackers" and the Mayor took the bullet intended for Roosevelt.

Roosevelt held Cermak in his arms on the way to Jackson Memorial Hospital, where his condition was diagnosed as critical. Cancelling the special train home, he stayed by Cermak's bedside and heard the Mayor whisper, "I'm glad it was me and not you. I wish you'd be careful. The country needs you."

Roosevelt told him, "The country needs men like you too, Tony."

Mrs. Joe H. Gill, wife of the president of Florida Power and Light, had been "lucky enough" to capture a front seat that night. She too was shot but recovered by March twentieth when the assailant, whose name was Giuseppe Zangora (he said he had "no use for the rich"), was electrocuted at Raiford Prison, held guilty of the murder of Mayor Cermak, who died on March sixth at Jackson Memorial Hospital.

Out of the tragic event came the bizarre instruction issued by the murderer: "Pusha da button." It came from a man in a hurry to leave this world. He had thought of killing President

The Governor of New York Alfred E. Smith observes Babe Ruth, Baseball's hero, try his hand at golf.

Hoover until he read in the newspaper that his successor was due in Miami.

The New Deal gave Florida on the whole a big push toward recovery, and by the end of 1933 banking in Florida had come through the depression. The winter of '34-'35 saw a jolly Christmas crowd piling into the Biltmore.

Journalist Heywood Broun brought his prep school son, Heyward Hale Broun, down for indoctrination into horse racing and jai-alai and Postmaster Jim Farley and his wife were on deck. Vacationing Edna Wallace Hopper, the exponent of perennial youth, was suggesting that everyone "should fall in love as much as possible," declaring that "an unhappy love affair is better than no love affair."

On the other hand, Ann Pennington, another perennial, slept all day in order to be fresh for her evening floor show appearance. The witty columnist Henry McLamore gave a hilarious impression of Pennington dancing.

The emphasis, of course, was on attracting out-of-towners to the hotel during the winter months, and the new strategy was much as the old: stage public events including tennis, golf,

Holding hands and bent on promotion are, left to right: a young Glenn Ford of motion pictures, Lyla Gorman Dix, Byoir publicist, columnist Dorothy Dey, Sonny Shepard of Wometco and Anna Sten, film actress.

beauty contests, tea dances without number, dinner dances, and aquatic events.

On the local scene, members of the Miami Biltmore Country Club had a glorious time with those Aerocars, which stopped at key places in town to pick up shoppers and transport them back home to Coral Gables. Back and forth traffic between the Roney and Biltmore was constant for ocean bathing at the Cabana Club.

Publisher George T. Delacorte, touting paperbacks as the wave of the future, brought his children down to soak up sun and establish an annual custom. The Junior League of Miami was staging "Jack and the Beanstalk" as a holiday contribution for children. Elizabeth Virrick was cast as the Balloon Man while Peg Delany Yonge (now Peg Holbein), played the Giant.

The National Congress of Parents and Teachers planned a Spring meeting, and the Biltmore was providing all kinds of services by installing audio-visual equipment; then, of course, there was all that glorious space, fifteen thousand feet of it, in which to place exhibits. This particular PTA congress was noted for the fact that three men were attending as delegates.

Nat Gubbins, the London columnist, came to write about

Film star Dorothy Lamour left her sarong at home when she came to visit the Biltmore.

what was going on and introduced a pre-luncheon drink at the Cascades Bar: half-port, half-brandy with a twist, no ice, served in a small wine glass. It was guaranteed to lull the senses and produce relaxation along with avoirdupois.

A pair of New York writers, Bill Corum and Quentin Reynolds, went back to their desks after a dip into the world of the Biltmore and, while reminiscing one evening at Twenty One, began to describe the drink to the bartender.

"Yeah," the fellow said, "They call it a Nat Gubbins."

They were dumfounded that news of the libation had preceded them and offered it as proof that Miami was definitely on the map.

The Miami Herald said it this way: "The annual invasion by winter visitors of Metropolitan Miami, outdoor sports capital of America and world's largest winter playground, is already in full swing."

There was one later item that kept Colonel Doherty chained to the Tower suite for a period. The Securities and Exchange Commission was investigating him, so it seemed best to stay out of sight. Carl Byoir resolved the tricky situation by having the Colonel appointed chairman for a series of the President's Birthday Balls to honor FDR and help wipe out polio. That seemed to call off the SEC.

The Colonel whiled away the period with a daily shave out on the balcony of the Tower Suite where once a week his barber, Pete Gulotti, gave him a haircut. The barber confessed much later that it was a nerve-wracking experience because the balcony was "very narrow and very high up" and sometimes "the wind was blowing," but that is where the Colonel decreed the event would take place.

Desi Arnaz made his first public appearance as an entertainer at the Biltmore while still in high school, and it was engineered by Jackie Ott. They were in the same history class at Miami High and got to be friends. Desi was in a school show and Jackie said, "Why don't you come over to the Miami Biltmore, and I'll see if my Dad can get you a spot with Johnny Silver." Desi did a Cuban number for his first engagement and later became "king of the conga line" at Miami Beach. When he began to talk about an actress named Lucille Ball out in California, Jackie Ott told him he'd "never heard of her."

"You will," Desi predicted.

New Year's Eve was slated to be a smash at the Biltmore, with a cast of entertainers that included Galli Galli, the Egyptian magician; and Pansy The Horse, a two-human comedy routine.

Hal Leyshon, managing editor of the *Miami Daily News*, had an idea for New Year's Eve: convey his Biltmore dinner party downtown to the News Tower to observe, as the clock struck midnight in Times Square, the first Wirephoto flashed from New York by the Associated Press.

Times Square was there all right, filled with masses celebrating the dawn of 1935 and here we all were in the land of eternal youth doing the same, joined by the magic of electronics. We rode through quiet streets, singing "Doodle-de-doo," Hal's favorite tune.

The whole nation was singing "Moon Over Miami," which was Number One on the Hit Parade, and "June in January" as George E. Merrick opened a new real estate office over at the Roney Plaza.

My office that season was just off the Palm Garden of the Roney where flamingos roamed freely. One day while my friend

I Love Lucille: so says the youthful Desi Arnaz, who made his debut as an entertainer at the Miami Biltmore.

Mildred Gilman was paying a visit, we saw a winter visitor with a bad case of frustration lift his foot and issue a resounding kick to the tropical bird's rear end. A Hearst writer whose book *Sob Sister* had sold to the movies, Mildred wrote about the flamingo incident for The *New Yorker*, calling her piece "Florida; Off Season."

Toward the end of the month, a burglary with built-in possibilities for a long-running newspaper story, scarcely the kind of publicity either Doherty or Byoir encouraged for the Biltmore, took place. Two men pointing revolvers entered the suite of Mrs. Margaret Hawkesworth Bell of New York. It was cocktail time and Mrs. Bell was entertaining Harry Content, also of New York. The burglars bound the pair hand and foot.

Because of the $250,000 estimated value of the jewelry removed from Mrs. Bell's room, Lloyds of London entered the picture, and their sleuths were not long in running down the culprits. They turned out to be known gangsters who in turn involved certain members of the Miami Police force.

No doubt this unfortunate incident was why, when several years later Evalyn Walsh McLean arrived wearing the Hope diamond, detectives were stationed outside her door during the entire stay. She wore the diamond bravely, and one of the funnier sights at a dinner dance was the parade of women slithering by her table in order to catch a glimpse of the gem which was said to carry bad luck along with its blazing beauty.

From 1931 to 1938 Colonel Doherty poured money into the Biltmore. Then, in failing health, he sold the controlling interest in the Florida Year Round Clubs to his friend George MacDonald, an associate in Cities Service, who was also on the board of directors of the Waldorf Astoria. It was an accommodation for Doherty, who died a year later.

Privately MacDonald called the Biltmore the "biggest white elephant" extant.

Westbrook Pegler, the columnist noted for his acerbity, dubbed it "a terrible turkey."

This is the Army

THE Japanese attack on Pearl Harbor on Dec. 7, 1941, remains a never-to-be-forgotten event for those who lived through it. We continue to recall what we were doing and saying and with whom that Sunday at the crucial moment when the word was flashed to the world. It changed lives and rang down the curtain on the parade of winter visitors to the Biltmore.

One of the rumors of the day was that the Crown Prince of Japan was playing golf at the Biltmore. Rumors turned to sharp and immediate reality when the Germans moved their submarines into our shipping lanes and lit up the South Florida sky with burning vessels. The first was in May when a Mexican tanker, the *Portera de Llano*, was torpedoed south of Fowey Rock and all the next day could be seen drifting north along the Gulf Stream. It was quickly followed by another hit on still another Mexican vessel, the *Faja de Oro*, after which Mexico declared war on Germany.

Morning bathers at Tahiti Beach, the spot created by George Merrick to provide bay swimming for his Biltmore guests, watched the ugly black globs of oil washing ashore and wondered exactly how far away South Florida actually was from the engulfing war.

Blackout curtains were ordered, an act that didn't do much if attack by air was being considered because that moon over Miami continued to shine on invitingly.

The Biltmore Tower lights were extinguished.

The season petered out. The last guest at the Biltmore that Spring of '42 was Secretary of State Cordell Hull.

Following its policy of annexing hotels in the area for military personnel and training of officers, the War Department pro-

67

ceeded to purchase the Miami Biltmore Hotel, and in November plans were announced for turning it into a regional station hospital. The government paid George MacDonald the sum of $895,000 for the structure built at a cost of ten million dollars sixteen years earlier.

Jack Thale of the *Miami Herald* made a sentimental journey to say farewell to the scene of so many glamorous and warm-hearted occasions and reported, "The welcome mat at the front door still proudly proclaims the Miami Biltmore but that's about all that's left."

There would be even less after the military was finished with it, and there would be days when the streets outside would receive piles of furnishings indiscriminately tossed out. Junk men would receive others. These were the original furnishings which had come from Wanamaker's and cost one million dollars.

Edward Millstone was one of the medical supply technicians assigned to "help turn the Biltmore into a hospital," and he was able to help himself to enough china and glassware to set up housekeeping with his bride. They actually had enough left over to last a lifetime. As Eddie watched the grandeur that was the Biltmore disappear, he also watched the favorite movie of the troops: *This Is The Army,* starring Ronald Reagan.

In a little while the military would be bringing in young men for medical checkouts before they were sent overseas.

One young man remembered fighting Eddie Swan "to a draw" back in the Biltmore during the depression days when he was a stripling entered in the Golden Gloves. The prize for these bouts was a ten dollar gift certificate at Turner's Sports Shop. This particular fellow saved up until he could buy a pair of ice skates. He's been in many a political battle since and in situations comparable to skating on thin ice, but he has held on to a wide political base as both Mayor of Miami and Mayor of all Dade County. His name: Stephen P. Clark.

As time went on, the hospital began to serve wounded soldiers and received a new name. In October 1944 it became Army Air Forces Regional Hospital (Twenty-eighth AAF Base Unit). On the same spot where the Merricks raised their tomatoes forty years before, hospital patients were raising hydroponic tomatoes for therapy. It was called "bathtub farming" and was taken up enthusiastically by recuperating soldiers.

George Merrick did not live to see the Biltmore taken over by the military. He died of a heart attack on March 26, 1942, at the age of fifty-six. The obituaries praised the man and referred to him as "one of the most remarkable men of his age." His sister Ethel said, "George was still paying off his debts when he died in 1942. He believed in Coral Gables until the day he died."

His record spoke for itself. In the late 1930s there had been a proposal to change the name of Coral Way, and Merrick wrote a letter to the City Commission protesting the idea.

"Since around 1900 the old portion of this old county highway has been known as Coral Way. It was the second road, back of the Bay, in the Miami area to be coral-rock-paved by the county, eight feet wide. LeJeune Road is the first . . . the name has character and distinctiveness."

Then there was the time someone had the bright idea that strings of colored lights would make a suitable adornment for one of the Coral Gables plazas. Denman Fink went to a meeting to protest and Merrick accompanied him. Finally he spoke up.

"If you put lights on the fountain you'll have to sell beer," he said. The idea lost favor.

Ethel was right.

He never gave up.

Merrick perhaps best demonstrated his strength of character in his final job as Postmaster. Henry Reno of the *Miami Herald* wrote: "Big, graying George E. Merrick, who during his heyday could wield his pen on a check for millions of dollars today becomes Miami's eleventh postmaster at a salary of $7,000 a year."

Allen Morris commented on the fact that "The years after the boom did not deal kindly with Merrick but he stood against adversity with unbowed head and beat his way back into a dominating position in the real estate field."

Merrick himself declared "The Coral Gables days were behind him," and in his new flower-decked office he promised "efficient and courteous service" and that he "would be no figurehead."

After a week on the job he said: "This is a $25 million business," and explained he was experiencing "a schooling" in what involved "stamp sales, mail delivery, banking, investment work, motor fleet operating and contract letting."

A flowery expression in print declared "this man of noble spirit looked forward to a future, not back to the past."

His funeral was impressive, but the way he plunged into the new job of Postmaster told a better story of the man.

Before he died he had the pleasure of viewing the mural created by Denman Fink in the building in which he worked as Postmaster: the Central Courtroom of the old Federal Courthouse and Post Office. In it Fink, following the habit of muralists to include known figures in their pieces, placed his nephew. Merrick is shown as young and brawny and is holding a crate of citrus fruit in his arms.

Under Lend Lease the University of Miami had been training young Englishmen in celestial navigation, housing them in the Anastasia building used in the first days of the university.

A poignant view of the former King of England, the Duke of Windsor, and then Governor General of the Bahamas, was offered on a day when he came from Nassau to inspect and meet with his former subjects.

The Duchess demonstrated her keen interest in Miami affairs when she and the Duke gave a joint press conference up in the Tower suite of the Biltmore. That day she astonished reporters by suggesting she had thought I was a brunette from my photograph used in my *Miami Herald* column, "Very Truly Yours." In the tiny photo I was wearing a turban which precluded identification by color of hair. Since none of us had been introduced by name to the Duchess this astonishment was justified and Mabel Frampton included it in her story in the *Miami News*. Wallis was definitely keeping an eye on the outside world, at least the nearest available in wartime.

Her pal and mentor, Lady Mendl, dislodged from France, had flown to Hollywood to enter a new life phase, and during wartime the film capital was simply out of bounds for the American-born Wallis Warfield. One of the observations of a sharp reporter was that Wallis had taken to wearing hair adornments that gave the impression of being crowns, quite in keeping with her husband's instructions that she should be addressed as Your Royal Highness.

There were all kinds of visitors to wartime Miami, and a woman of completely opposite makeup and capacity was First

It's not the Tower of London but the Biltmore Tower and it is being occupied by the ex-King of England. The Duke of Windsor and his American born Duchess.

Lady Eleanor Roosevelt, who swept in for a brief visit and made a whirlwind tour which included a stop at the Biltmore hospital. She left those of us trailing her that day down below while she took the elevator to visit the recuperating soldiers. The next move was to join a cavalcade of automobiles bound for Overtown where a group of blacks awaited. Here again I did not go unrecognized and mention it as confirmation of something that was world accepted: Mrs. Roosevelt was not only sharp, but caring.

I had spent hours back in Westchester County following her around when she was campaigning for FDR for Governor. I was writing for the Macy chain of newspapers and later was one of a group to visit her Manhattan townhouse after her husband was elected President. That day we were shown samples of the furniture being turned out in her ValKill factory. In connection with the Goddard Settlement House benefit before I left New York in '34, the meetings had been brief and perfunctory. Certainly she would not be expected to pick me out of a crowd of pressing reporters waiting for her in the lobby of the old Miami Biltmore after so long a time.

But she did.

As she emerged from the elevator she caught my eye and stopped short. In a quick moment she wanted to know how things went with me and asked, "Do you have any children?"

"Two daughters," I told her, "one coming down with chicken pox." She pressed my hand before moving on.

In mid-May of 1946 the Army took over the Miami Biltmore, and it was renamed Pratt General Hospital in honor of Col. Fabian L. Pratt, a pioneer Army Air Corps surgeon.

One of the hospital's claims to fame would be that General Dwight D. Eisenhower slept in the Tower suite.

Martin Fine, a leading Miami citizen stationed there at the time, recalls that "the golf course was being manicured by every man able to stand on his feet" in preparation for Ike's visit.

A group of Miami doctors, many returned from active military service, served as civilian consultants. The women of the community, who had answered the call of the Red Cross to serve as Gray Ladies when the first wave of the seriously wounded from Anzio were flown in, continued to serve throughout the hospital era of the Biltmore. They wrote letters, ran errands, and took the men for walks in wheelchairs, often driving them to their homes for short visits when the men were up to it. Roxie Walters, Jo Willis, Helen Lewis and Grace Toomey were a stout nucleus of the group.

Historically more important than the future president of the United States being an occupant of the Tower or the lengthy occupancy of the Veterans Administration is the fact that it was at the Biltmore that the School of Medicine of the University of Miami was born.

It was not exactly an easy birth. The complications involved the Florida Legislature and voices from all over the state as various cities vied for the privilege of launching the first medical school in Florida. It was the only state in the South without one, and every time a Florida student went to medical school out of state, it cost the taxpayers fifteen hundred dollars a year.

Dr. Bowman F. Ashe, the outstanding president of the University of Miami, whose skill and determination held the institu-

Amputees from World War II show their medals and pose with Gray Ladies. Left is Mrs. Humphrey (Grace) Toomey; Mrs. Hillard (Josephine) Willis right. Unidentified entertainer stands by.

tion together during the perilous times following the collapse of the boom and for decades thereafter, was strongly in favor of establishing a School of Medicine. On April 18, 1947, the Board of Trustees agreed.

An opening of the new department as early as October was considered, but when the announcement was made public, it caused a royal brouhaha of such proportions that the University of Miami withdrew its plans and went so far as to take out an advertisement in the *Miami Herald* to tell the world it had.

The Dade delegation of State Legislators wrote a letter to Dr. Ashe declaring that if Florida failed to get the state-supported medical school for which it was pushing (with vocal support from both the City of Miami and the Miami Chamber of Commerce), the blame would be placed squarely at the door of Dr. Ashe and the University of Miami.

A bill to establish a medical and dental college in Dade County as a branch of the University of Florida had already been placed before the legislature, and the City of Miami had offered land near Jackson Memorial Hospital for a site.

Out of all this, who would ever think that the Medical School would ultimately be housed in the exact spot George Merrick had considered for the University site before he built the Biltmore?

It took a suit before the Florida Supreme Court to bring it to fruition.

In point of fact the first medical school in Florida was the Tallahassee College of Medicine and Surgery, which opened in 1883. Two years after that it was moved to Jacksonville where, a year later, it folded.

So did the 1947 plan for a state-funded school of medicine but a year later the University of Miami took a step that would put it back in line for getting a school started, although it was not evident at the time.

Dr. Leonard G. Roundtree of the Mayo Clinic, who had retired to Miami Beach where the United States Veterans' Hospital was then located at the former Nautilus Hotel, proposed a program that brought him into the picture. His idea was to establish a graduate training and research project, preferably tied in with the University of Miami.

Geography cast the final vote. The Veterans establishment was moved to the Biltmore in Coral Gables and the Miami-Veterans Medical Research Unit brought the board of trustees and Doctor Ashe back to the drawing board with plans for a medical school. After a piece of legislation was patiently engineered by State Senator R. B. (Bunn) Gautier, the School of Medicine was born five years later with the blessing of city officials, the Chamber of Commerce, and the state. Dr. Ashe was jubilant.

The Dade County Medical Association publication, *The Bulletin*, carried a message from its editor, Dr. Franz H. Stewart, for the twenty-eight students starting medical careers on the twenty-second of September 1952. Dr. Stewart, who also served as chairman pro tem of medicine in the new school, wrote:

"There should be no great excitement. Important developments mark important dates on the calendar only after time has added memory, satisfaction and pride. . . . These students will be remembered according to the humanity and the impetus to work and study they carry from the school."

These first students carried from the school memories of a special sort. They were occupying a separate building which had begun life as servants' quarters for the old Biltmore. Small bedrooms, which had provided sinks and running water, were opened up after walls were knocked down. This explained why there was a sink at the end of every stack of books in the library.

Furthermore, the reason those first students often took off their shoes and put their feet on the table during lectures has a logical explanation as well. The lecture room was below ground level and opened into a patio. When the rains were heavy, the water washed into the lecture room. You don't have to be a medical student to realize that sitting around with wet feet is not conducive to good health.

Upstairs in the laboratory Dr. Nancy L. Noble, who had come from Emory University to join the faculty, remembers that there was no money to purchase a proper drain, so a garden hose attached to a circulating water pump was improvised. There were times when someone would forget to turn off the pump, and water would drip down into the classroom below where Dr. George Paff was teaching anatomy. The word was spread that the med school might not yet be the best, but it was well on its way to being the cleanest.

In December Bowman Ashe died. He had fought hard to bring the Medical School to his university, and today it has an enviable reputation all over the world.

It certainly wasn't easy to run either a medical school or a hospital in the old Biltmore. For a hospital the corridors were much too narrow, there was no air conditioning; and, in addition, it cost half a million dollars a year to keep up.

Beginning with World War II, radical changes had been put into effect, such as filling in a section of the swimming pool with concrete, blocking out windows with concrete blocks, and providing fire escapes. Luxuries had been snatched away. Fluorescent lighting had replaced ornate chandeliers. Overall layers of muted-military favored gray and white had made the old Biltmore scarcely recognizable. Nixon Smiley wrote the sight of it was "depressing, the feeling one has after attending a funeral."

Dr. Mary Lou Lewis interned at Jackson Memorial Hospital in 1967, and part of her training was to serve at the Veterans Hospital. "I never saw any pretty parts of the old hotel," she said. "I guess they were all covered up with wall boards. Interning is a trial by fire for everybody but that was the worst part of mine. All I remember are very sick patients and very narrow hallways."

When the Veterans Administration closed its operation and moved to suitable new quarters close by Jackson Memorial Hospital in March of 1968, it was the end of another era and many thought the end of the Biltmore itself.

Celebrating a reunion weekend at the restored Biltmore, the Medical Alumni Association looked back and, echoing Dr. Lewis, one after the other exclaimed: "I didn't know all this beautiful building was part of it." They were celebrating the thirty-fifth anniversary of the founding of the School of Medicine that weekend of March 6-8, 1987, during which a commemorative plaque was placed in the lobby. Verily, they had all come a long way, along with the Biltmore. Now they had the plaque to mark the spot.

Save the Biltmore

THE City of Coral Gables announced the establishment of the Biltmore Development Board three months after the Veterans Administration moved out.

The next month W. H. Philbrick led a group with the rallying cry, *Save The Biltmore.* The Biltmore was now part of the General Services Administration (GSA) of the federal government, and the purpose of the new board was to protect the property from inappropriate development.

Helen Wells, writing in the *Herald's* society pages, called an "SOS for a landmark" and went on to praise The Villagers which she described as "those stalwart femmes who saved the Douglas Entrance now working to save the old Biltmore hotel." In a few months The Villagers announced "a Tea Dance at the Biltmore" to plead their cause.

Before too long, however, the question would arise—erupt would be a better word— Save the Biltmore, but for *what* and for *whom?*

As far back as 1947 the City of Coral Gables had been able to arrange a lease to take over the Biltmore golf course and in September 1966 was successful in purchasing it. (Seventeen holes of the thirty-six hole course had been sold earlier to the Riviera Country Club.)

Moreover, as far back as 1942 when the United States government acquired the Biltmore, the City of Coral Gables had made known the fact that it wanted first dibs on the property should the government ever decide to dispose of it.

W. Keith Phillips, Jr., who served on the Commission for a decade from 1963 to 1973, the last two years of his terms as Mayor of Coral Gables, remained consistent in his efforts to bring about the return of the entire Biltmore property of close to

77

twenty acres to the people of Coral Gables. He had met George Merrick as a small boy and felt himself to be very much a part of the Coral Gables dream. His father had also served as Mayor of the Gables.

The scenario that evolved after GSA contracted to turn over the 19.8 acres of the Biltmore property to a developer, Maston G. O'Neal, proved as convoluted as any event connected with the boomtime hotel.

The O'Neal plan was to build high-rise condominiums and offices on the Biltmore property. He had been introduced to GSA officials in Atlanta by the chairman of the Biltmore Development Board, Michael Tobin.

Before the furor was resolved, a number of fascinating things happened. A GSA official, traveling incognito, attended a City Commission meeting, where he sat throughout a discussion in which his name was frequently mentioned. His name was Thomas Gherardi and not Mr. Smith, as indicated that evening. Then there was the meeting when O'Neal rose to his feet and announced his financial backers "had more money than God."

A congressional investigation was followed by a ruling by the Justice Department and signed by William D. Ruckelshaus, assistant attorney general, in favor of the acquisition of the property by Mr. O'Neal "since he has agreed to preserve the Tower of the former Biltmore Hotel and other parts of the property for public use."

Aroused public opinion included the expressed fear that the developer would have the legal right to "demolish the Tower and its very existence would be at his whim."

Like nearly everyone else, it seemed, Mr. Ruckelshaus had not been fully informed. The developer, when pressed, had promised to give the Country Club to the city but reneged almost immediately. However, he had promised to keep the light burning in the Tower.

The Tower seemed more significant than the whole 19.8 acres.

When O'Neal indicated he would build two more towers around the additional cluster of structures, who knows what arousing effect it had on the citizens of Coral Gables?

One who was in the thick of the fray during the 1970s with the GSA-Coral Gables encounter was Donald Lebrun who as assistant city manager was assigned to Mayor Phillips to keep

track of the fast-moving events. Later he would be the fulltime
city manager and see the Biltmore scenario unfold. In the
1970s his assignments were as varied as attending key meetings in Washington and Atlanta and measuring parking places
to prove to the GSA that the Gables was equal to taking on the
Biltmore.

Looking back on the turbulent early 1970s, Mayor Phillips
says that he "made a vow to expend every effort to acquire the
Biltmore for the City so that its citizens could determine the
destiny of the property. . . ."

So, he declares, did M. Lewis Hall, Jr., and Charles B. Knisk-
ern. Both were lawyers and together they engaged the legal
services of Parker D. Thomson to bring suit in federal court to
abrogate the agreement between O'Neal and the GSA. As the
case continued, it became a fervent cause with a number of
lawyers giving their time and energies on a volunteer basis.
Robert L. Koeppel, who fought Tobin on the Development
Board, was elected chairman after Tobin's resignation and
played a strong leadership role. He stirred things up by going to
Washington; and in the first two months of 1971, the board
recommended that the City condemn O'Neal's interest in the
Biltmore contract and pay the developer $140,000 in order to
acquire the property for public use. The Commission endorsed
the board's recommendation.

It did not go all that smoothly. There was personal gain of a
noteworthy sort involved, and a political faction stood firmly
behind the developer. The newspapers began to clamor, de-
manding access to some of the GSA documents. United States
Congressman Dante Fascell and Senator Claude Pepper ended
up providing office space to delegations arriving in Washington
for huddles with government officials.

The O'Neal deal involved a land swap, and the *Herald* editori-
alized by suggesting "the feds find the $2.5 million necessary to
buy those five sites in Georgia and Carolina and leave the
Biltmore property to the people of Coral Gables." It called the
deal "a manipulation . . . in one of the finest residential areas in
America."

In another editorial it declared, "the Biltmore chickens from
Coral Gables have come home to roost in Washington. . . ."

The *Miami News* disclosed that O'Neal, whose deal with the
GSA was, as already stated, for $2.59 million, was also dicker-

ing for a sale with the Florida Bible College for what he was calling a "giveaway price of $3.6 million."

There were others standing in line to put in bids for the Biltmore, one being Florida International University.

As 1971 dawned, City Attorney Charles Spooner gave an "off-the-cuff-opinion."

"I seriously doubt that our public use would be greater than that of the federal government," he said.

That wasn't the way the fighting lawyers and their children saw it. Leon Black and his wife Maggie, both lawyers, enlisted the services of their offspring to go out and collect signatures of voters requesting the GSA to sell to the city. Their children— David, Becky, and Julia— went roaring forth, along with the Parker Thomson tribe of Parker, Jamie, and Meg and the Koeppel children, Rob, Steve, and Peyton.

They formed a brigade and spread themselves throughout the Gables, stationed themselves on key arteries of traffic, and plunged into the fight with youthful enthusiasm.

A newspaper photograph of them with a sign asking the plaintive question, "Didn't there used to be a golf course around here?" greeted newspaper readers. Radio and television took up the cry to save the Biltmore.

The two-pronged approach plotted by the lawyers— to sue the government and arouse the voters— began to pay off; then they managed to get a three million dollar bond issue on the April ballot for the city to buy the Biltmore.

Little hope was held out at City Hall for its success but when the votes were counted it went sailing through. So did the one-million-dollar request to buy the Country Club. Out of ten issues put before the voters seven failed. The lawyers of Coral Gables rode off on their white horses and celebrated a victory in which their children shared. They had done a good deal of the leg work while their parents were making a living downtown. The bulky files tell an exciting story.

It was only part of a happy ending and marked the beginning of a series of forward events. Days after Phillips became Mayor, the city joined in the suit being brought against the government.

They won it.

In response to the court action, the government in the last days of 1971 declared the Biltmore properties surplus, thereby opening the door for Coral Gables to apply to purchase.

Coral Gables High School students pitch in to clear up the deserted Miami Biltmore Country Club in order to hold their Senior Prom there.

They wouldn't be needing that three million dollars for the Biltmore after all.

They wouldn't have to buy it.

The government would give it to them.

President Richard Nixon's Legacy of Parks program and the Historic Monument Act in 1972 led the way for an official ceremony on April 21, 1973, in which Julie Nixon Eisenhower conveyed the Biltmore deed to Mayor Robert B. Knight with former Mayor Phillips an active participant. Historian Arva Moore Parks had been a key figure in working to have the Biltmore declared an historical monument. Clearly she had an interest in the matter.

"My father courted my mother at the Biltmore," she said.

While the Biltmore Development Board and the City of Coral Gables stewed over what to do next about the Biltmore, a senior at Coral Gables High School named Tom Pepper came up with an idea.

Why not get all the service clubs together on a common project to benefit the community and at the same time raise money by holding the senior prom at the beautiful old Country Club?

A third generation Miamian, Tom grew up in the Gables and from his grandparents, the John Lawrence Peppers, learned about the glamour days. They were founding members of the Country Club and, like many others, held the Biltmore high in their affections.

The idea took hold, and a Roaring '20s Senior Prom was planned for May 1974— but first there was the matter of cleaning up the old building. They marched in with sledge hammers and removed what the military had created, "a building within a building." "We must have put in two thousand hours," Pepper recalls. "The project caught the imagination of the community and we got lots of assistance but we did all the demolition work, the plastering and painting ourselves."

It also caught the attention of the media worldwide and, to their surprise, the students began receiving Biltmore memorabilia from people everywhere.

The night of the Prom there were antique cars and girls dressed in the spirit of the 1920s and it was an all-round success story. Two senior proms were held there.

Taking their cue from the students, the Beaux Arts, a support group of the Lowe Gallery of the University of Miami, decided to stage an elaborate ball there. In the Fall of 1974 members rolled up their sleeves and went to work to make the old country club attractive for the occasion.

Rosalind (Mrs. Philippe) Moore was chairman and recalls that the cocktails downstairs and dinner and dancing upstairs provided a background "of grace and beauty and was a terrific success."

The long-running serial of saving the Biltmore was in no danger of cancellation, and in October 1975 the Metropolitan Museum and Art Center of Coral Gables reached an agreement with the City to move into the Biltmore Country Club.

Renovations began with government money to transform the building into a museum and school for the arts. The ballroom, scene of so many lavish events, was turned into gallery and office space. Classrooms were placed on the ground floor.

The museum group had started out with three sponsors in 1960. They were Artist Elizabeth Upham Davis, Patty McNaughton, and Allie McDanald who formed a workshop at the

Beaux Arts Ball chairman Mrs. Philippe (Rosemond) Moore, holds the fan; her sister, Mrs. James Bowler, was co-chairman.

Lowe Gallery, then moved into a warehouse provided by the tycoon Arthur Vining Davis. Now it was starting a new life with a new name. It was dedicated on Feb. 17, 1980, at a ceremony presided over by Joan Mondale, wife of Vice-President of the United States Fritz Mondale.

Six months later the curator, Michael Spring, wrote in *The Biltmore Revisited* on the occasion of a stirring photo-documentary exhibition of *The Miami Biltmore Hotel and Country Club* that John McEntee Bowman half a century before had made a prediction: "Fifty years from now there will be a successor to the Biltmore and there will be a group of men like ourselves reciting the memories of this occasion, looking over photographs, perhaps and hailing us as among the pioneers of Coral Gables. I am proud to be in such a company."

The "company" continued to increase with the formation of the Center for Latin and American Arts and Studies (CLASS) in 1979, adding a dimension to the museum.

Five years later a group of young professionals of different backgrounds and different areas of interest added their voices under the name Junior Committee.

But the whole story wasn't written yet.

In the summer of 1987 a new idea was being introduced: a merger of the Lowe Gallery of the University of Miami and the Metropolitan Museum with Ira Licht of the Lowe running the show and under an entirely new name. A serious proposal, it would return the Country Club to the City of Coral Gables within a five year period. If it happens, it would put the two structures back together for a common purpose and restore the complete Biltmore as envisioned by George Merrick.

Race with the Clock

THE rescue of the Country Club only served to point up the sad decay of the once imposing hotel.

Pigeons made the Biltmore their home. Vandals came and took away pieces of her. A few foxes, left over from Merrick's grandiose plan to introduce riding to hounds, prowled the premises.

City officials and members of the Biltmore Development Board wrestled with one proposal after another, casting about for the proper solution of what to do with this wreck of a structure now designated an historic monument.

In mid-January 1983 a committee appointed by the city listened to presentations by six finalists in what had become spirited bidding for the privilege of restoring the old hotel.

Plans differed. One called for converting the hotel into 232 luxury apartments after changing its original concept of housing for the elderly to the middle-aged in order to suit the tastes of the committee. Another proposal was for guests suites, with office space and an international studies center for the University of Miami. The latter seemed a highly creative adaptation, but the presentation of developer Earl Worsham and architect Richard Rose, proved the most eye-catching.

Rose opened with a quote from a poem by George Merrick: "There's a land that always calls me and that draws me more and more . . . " The *Miami Herald* used a half column cut of the late Mr. Merrick in its coverage.

It wasn't until mid-September that a decision was made. The job went to Worsham and Rose.

Elizabeth Morgan, writing in the *Herald* on September fifteenth, declared "the clock starts ticking for the restoration" and pointed out the terms of the deal which gave the developers, among other things, six months to secure financing. It was the beginning of a major project which would bring into the Biltmore's cast of characters a new face, a new presence, a man who might well have sat down with George Merrick and they would have understood each other fully.

It was said of Merrick that he seemed remote, and the same might be said of a young architectural conservator named Joseph L. Herndon. He was selected to play the role of project manager in the huge undertaking which would test everyone's abilities and patience for three years and beyond.

It would take another two years before the city would finally sign a lease with Worsham Brothers under a new name—the Coral Gables Biltmore Corporation with Worsham the principal partner and Rose reduced to a limited partner role. Now the need to watch the clock would become crucial because the forty-seven million dollar cost for the restoration was being assisted by federal laws permitting investors to receive tax credits for restoring historic landmarks. This law carried certain requirements, one being that the job must be completed during the year 1986. The Biltmore was to be the largest tax-free project in the United States that year.

Joseph Herndon is one of a new breed of individuals, almost priest-like in his devotion to the cause of preservation. In addition he carries a double-edged sword because he has become an astute business man, dealing with banks and contractors on a regular basis. His aim is, he says, to yank preservation into the mainstream of the competitive world of business.

Recognition for restoring the Old Post Office in Washington, D.C. and projects as diverse as a sixteenth century palace in Saudi Arabia and a two and a half century building in Pascagoula, Mississippi—the old Spanish fort—have placed him, at the age of thirty-seven, as an authority in his field. It is a field for which he prepared himself by obtaining a graduate degree from Columbia University's School of Architecture and Planning, and later studying at London's Bedford College, seat of the Victorian Society of Great Britain. He started out as a history teacher in his home state of Tennessee and, since switching careers, has been involved in eighty restorations.

The Biltmore is his favorite despite long months of frustrating bureaucratic and community-inspired delays before ever getting started. By late July 1985 Herndon said mildly, "We thought we'd be done by now and have guests in there."

Joseph Herndon, project manager of the Biltmore restoration, a true believer in the preservation movement.

Neighbors were claiming that the plans had altered considerably since first presented and quarreled over the fact that the number of rooms, increased from 196 to 285, would demand increased parking space. "The neighbors have bad memories of parked cars all over when it was a hospital," Herndon commented.

The developers had been pushing right along for some office space, but the city had set its sights on a luxury hotel, period. Herndon explained: "Hotels typically lose money the first five years because of the tremendous start-up costs, . . . office space covers those expenses." He added: "The founder was a dreamer, a lovely dreamer. He had great visions and enchanting ideas. The city doesn't want to lose any of that."

The optimistic view was that construction would begin by Christmas if the developers were able to obtain the variances they needed from the city. State and federal approval were expected to be no problem. That done, the financing could proceed.

The color of the Biltmore turned out to be the liveliest and most heated controversy in connection with the entire restoration. It became a headline item in the Fall of '86 as protests poured into the city and the area newspapers in the form of letters to the editor. The people made known in no uncertain terms that a sentimental attachment existed for the sixty-year-old structure, the original color of which, they insisted, was a soft pink and not the miserable, shocking, unlovely brown-tinged shade arrived at by the restorers and called burnt orange. The military had plastered gray and white over the surface but those who remembered it as a center of life said sharply that the color being used on the mammoth building was not acceptable.

Mayor Dorothy Thomson termed it "a dismal brown" while a former Mayor, James Dunn, declared it to be "barnyard brown." He added, "I've heard it called a lot worse."

Ellen Uguccioni, historic preservation administrator for Coral Gables, had her hands full at the receiving end of the outcry. She went before the Historic Board of the City of Coral Gables on two occasions to have the color approved. Samples of various shades had been placed on five locations of the building considered the most protected areas, for purposes of accurate matching with the original. All this was to give the board a choice after experts in Tallahassee had established their findings. With microscope and scalpel they had probed straight through to the original paint job and come up with what they established as a fairly exact mixture of the original color.

Tell that to Loretta Sheehy, or Jean Kitchens, or Lyla Gorman Dix who, one way or another were closely connected with the Biltmore in its early days. They all wrote impassioned letters denouncing the color chosen.

The Kitchens letter— in The *Miami Herald*— referred to her late husband, Dr. F. E. Kitchens, who had served as the first health officer in the Gables as well as being team physician for the first University of Miami football game. She wrote as follows:

"I'm certain if he were here he would concur with me that the Biltmore's original color was pink— not flamingo or shocking pink, but a soft, soothing pastel pink."

Then there was Richard Rose, the prime mover in getting the

Biltmore on the road to restoration. Asked his opinion, he gave a truly colorful answer.

"The Biltmore is a female building and pale pink is a female color whereas burnt orange is a male color." He quoted the Contessa de Pucci as his source.

Today the sun glitters on the burnt orange, which is striking and offers a fine new face for the Biltmore.

But it certainly isn't pink. How do I recall it?

Tannish pink!

Two people who worked steadily to help preserve both the Biltmore and the Gables went before the City Commission just before Christmas. Their mission was to request financial assistance to re-paint the adjoining museum the same burnt orange in order to conform and, while they were at it, make use of the visiting Mexican artisans to work on its faded frieze.

Keith Phillips, who as mayor had gone to Washington to request acquisition of the Biltmore, made his point.

"We can't leave the former clubhouse standing like a sore thumb."

Arva Parks backed him up. "It's like having one new shoe and one old shoe."

It was figured the paint job would cost forty-seven thousand dollars, while restoration of the frieze would run about fifty-three thousand dollars. The city gave the money with a wistful comment that the museum, which occupied the old country club for ten dollars a year, might consider putting a little money in the kitty. The museum commented that it was in financial trouble.

Herndon declared himself to be "pleased as punch" at the strong reactions toward the paint job.

Herndon prepared himself for the Biltmore job with intense research in New York and Washington, D. C. libraries, examining all the Schultze and Weaver sketches and plans, reading any and all material on the period. One of the results of his research, an article on "How to Make Fake Travertine," proved a find because the travertine trim used in the Biltmore turned out to be fake.

What was it like the first time he walked into the deserted and ill-treated relic of past glory days in November of 1982?

"It was morning, a sunny day," he recalls. I came in through

Restoration of the Biltmore was a mammoth job.

a temporary entrance on the lower floor where the window now is— it was a walkway for the handicapped."

Was it a challenge he felt?

"No. It was obvious what they had done. The majority of my work was un-doing— no time for laments. I came through that dinky doorway into a grand hotel . . . the stench of pigeon droppings . . . the vandalism marks were all there . . . but I saw it all as it should be."

The lobby?

"The basics were gone but there was no mystery for me. As in other projects, it was clear to me from the first day. . . . "

Herndon calls the Mediterranean style with which he was dealing day after day, driving toward a 1986 Biltmore opening, "boastful eclecticism."

There is nothing boastful about Herndon. In hard-hat and work clothes he was all over the place with the crew, balancing himself on the scaffolds surrounding the tower, climbing up with the Mexican artists he imported to bring back the blue star-hung ceilings in the lobby, checking every inch of the work.

"I know every craftsman who did each job. I get good work— and I might add a good price." His eyes glistened. "Mostly I enjoy working with skilled, dedicated people."

Artisans at work restoring the main lobby of the Biltmore.

He failed to add that assisting with passports and arranging lodgings fell under his jurisdiction and that a normal working day for him was eighteen hours.

Is the preservation movement a statement of protest against a throwaway society? He answers this way: "Some of us hope to prove another element in our society. . . . There is a past as well as a future."

It was Herndon who led me into the tiled floor of what had been George Merrick's office up in the tower. The hotel had been open three months, but now there were legal entanglements involving sub-contractors and the threat of foreclosure.

Then I remembered something he'd said earlier about the population having doubled in his own lifetime and all at once I felt I understood his goals and what he meant when he said, "You have to show physical results. Words do not count. There is a definite physical core . . . "

I thought of poetry-loving George Merrick determinedly setting out to create an entire city that would be balanced, creating a new art form almost— and I knew that George Merrick and

Joseph Herndon would understand each other quite thoroughly. Particularly when Herndon said, "The fact that this world can produce a project like this gives us hope."

The amount of complicated art restoration and sheer back-breaking, clean-up work required to finish the job on time was staggering. The quality of the work was magnificent; the problems were enormous.

An elaborate press party planned to introduce the media to the restored Biltmore had to be moved to a tent because the certificate of occupancy was not yet approved by the city. A second party given for the bank which lent twenty-seven million dollars for the project had to take place under tent as well.

Then, there was the matter of the fire of suspicious origin which broke out on the sixth floor of the Biltmore prior to the re-opening and was dealt with promptly and efficiently by the water sprinkler system.

The system worked so effectively it sent thousands of gallons of water shooting all the way down to the restored lobby, causing damage estimated at more than one hundred thousand dollars. The damage to the psyches of artisans restoring the lobby was not estimated easily.

When it came right down to the wire the first signed up guests for the day after Christmas grand reopening had to be turned away and sent by limousines with baskets of fruit to a downtown hotel.

Not an auspicious beginning for the reincarnation of the Biltmore, but technically the deadline was met when officials and several die-hard lovers of the Biltmore, among them Keith Phillips and his wife, spent the first night under the tower.

In large headlines before the re-opening, the *Miami News* in its "Money" section called the restoration "a beautiful gamble." So it proved to be for Earl Worsham, who in a re-shuffling after court action lost control of the Biltmore. He will be remembered for being the instrument for putting the Biltmore back together.

Up in New York there were no more meetings under the clock because preservationists lost the battle to save the Biltmore, but in Coral Gables the Biltmore was standing tall, not the tallest building in Florida, but surely the most tested and enduring.

Enduring as well were the memories collected by the Country Club families. They ranged all the way from mingling with the offspring of winter visitors at the Biltmore nursery school to roller skating down the sweeping hotel ramp on summer days when northern visitors were absent.

Then there was the time when Patty Weiland was hit by a golf ball delivered by Patty Berg at the second hole, and the never-to-be-forgotten Fourth of July when one of the men shooting off the brilliant fireworks display blew himself up in front of the shocked onlookers.

The night the fish tanks in the Cascades Bar exploded is still another tale, this one told with gusts of laughter.

They are all part of the fabric of memory woven over six decades.

Now a new set of memories is in the process of being created, and proof that the old wheel of life has turned since the 1960s when marriage ceremonies were inclined toward the unorthodox, there is a flocking of brides to the Biltmore for wedding receptions and often the ceremony itself.

Frank Thorn, general manager and vice president of the hotel, reports that bride bookings began to pour in at the instant of the reopening and that they continue at a fast clip with a sellout through Christmas.

One who has a clear view of it all is Linda Joyce. She is what is known as a "banquet server." I fell to chatting with her as she stood behind a food table at a recent wedding reception.

"It is interesting to see how elaborate they are," she pointed out. "It is as though the palatial hotel gives brides something they have been pining for, something they hope to hold on to for the rest of their lives."

German-born Peter Rose, representing 180 elegant independent hotels all over the world, came to look in on the Biltmore after its re-creation. We sat having coffee in the patio where, so very much out of place, electronic rock and roll music blasted the night air.

He was saying: "It takes a year to eliminate management problems." He spoke of the "renaissance of old hotels worldwide as part of a nostalgic wave" and the fact that it is stronger here in the USA than anyplace else.

Then he added gently, "But then Europe did not intentionally destroy its beautiful buildings. An act of war did."

The Preservation Ball

THEY rolled out the red carpet, donned finery from the roaring twenties; and sixty one years and one day after the historical opening of the Miami Biltmore, they danced to "When the Moon Shines in Coral Gables" all over again.

It was January 16, 1987, and the old hotel was abloom with lights, music, action, and the quaffing of wine.

A menu patterned after the original opening was printed on a replica of the elaborate oversized 1926 menu with the same flag-draped photographs of Merrick and Bowman and the list of tempting food: Coupe Andalouse followed by Turtle Soup, Poached Halibut Parsley Noilly Prat Sauce, Medallion of Veal with Foie Gras, Truffle Armagnac Sauce, and on into the salad, ending with Fresh Strawberries Romanoff.

The souvenir menu also carried the same immortal words of Dr. Crane: "Many people may come and go but this structure will remain a thing of lasting beauty."

The stage was set once again. Who cared that the billing mistakenly credited "Moon Over Miami" as the song of the 1920s? That song of the mid-1930s was also a part of the heritage. It belonged with "When the Moon Shines In Coral Gables," introduced by Jan Garber decades earlier.

Brilliant searchlights played back and forth on the illuminated Giralda Tower. Doormen in top hats and white gloves greeted guests who began arriving up the ramp, some in antique cars, the ladies in beads and feathers, the men in black tie. Medieval trumpeters sounded an official welcome.

Off to the right as one entered the lobby stood the proud receiving line made up of developers and preservationists, beaming at the sellout crowd.

The Preservation Ball chairman, Dora Valdez-Fauli and her husband Coral Gables Commisioner Raul Valdes-Fauli, beam approval at the success of the event.

Lowe Museum director Ira Licht congratulates Mrs. Gerald (Marty) Stofik, president of the Dade Heritage Trust, while Sharon Clark looks on.

J. Jackson Walter, president of the National Trust for Historic Preservation, stands in the receiving line with Mrs. James R. (Sallye) Jude, president of the Florida Trust for Historic Preservation.

All of 650 responded to invitations so quickly it was necessary to send back checks— history repeating itself.

Taking bows along with the chairman, Dora Valdes-Fauli, were the preservationist-presidents whose groups would benefit from the event: Mrs. Marty Lee Stofik of Dade Heritage Trust, Sallye Jude of the Florida Trust for Historic Preservation, and J. Jackson Walter, National Trust for Historic Preservation. It was one occasion when a receiving line was a genuine part of the excitement.

Only fifteen years old, the preservation movement had gained followers in record numbers. This particular event, satisfying as it did the increasing thirst for elegance and nostalgia on the part of Americans, was cause for extra jubilation. The Biltmore revival was being compared to the restorations of The Willard Hotel in Washington, D.C. and the saving of Grand Central Station in New York.

In the words of Mr. Walter, "Preservation is emerging as a major force."

Return of the 20s is exemplified in the women's costumes at the ball. Left to right: Ruth Wackenhut, Roger Ward and Joan Wackenhut-Ward.

Actually, it was emerging as a multi-billion dollar industry having a large impact on American life. People like Herndon and Ellen Ugucionni were members of a cult almost, a cult organized not a moment too soon when one thinks of the Roney Plaza being turned into a pile of dust without any weapons to halt the bulldozer.

At the ball Ellen was showing a film about the restoration, a running account of what it involved. What it did not show was her lugging heavy camera equipment including battery packs, climbing clear to the Tower, fighting dust and dozens of dead pigeons, ducking under girders in stairwells— all to get the whole wonderful story of the return of the Biltmore to the land of the living.

Paul Whiteman was not among those present that night, but The Billy Rolle orchestra was and played old tunes to a group of mixed-generation dancers, all caught up in a common mood of shared fervor. At one spot on the terrace, Paco del Puerto's Flamenco Dancers held forth. There was a moment when the wife of retired Dr. John W. Dix, urged on by the musicians, did a solo number. As Lyla Gorman, back in her University of Miami student days, she had launched a career as part of the Carl Byoir organization and knew her way around the old Biltmore.

*Eunice Merrick. "She never
lost her tinkly laugh ..."*

There never had been a better party, not even back in 1926, it was generally agreed. The gondoliers weren't missed at all—but then, they were part of the scene in memory.

Grandmothers and young matrons crowded the terrace dance floors, wearing headbands and Paris gowns that had been tucked away in trunks for sixty years. As in the first opening, all the men seemed handsome and graceful as the glow of a more carefree time settled over the place that had all but disappeared and now miraculously was brought back to life.

Joe Herndon, casting aside hard hat and sneakers for a tuxedo, predicted: "With age, the Biltmore will only become more graceful and enduring."

A few blocks away from the celebration to mark the emergence of the Biltmore from limbo, Eunice Merrick got out and examined some of the designer gowns she had worn during the heady period of the 1920s.

Placing them on a bed she stood back and wondered.

Was it the peach beaded chiffon—or was it the black lace she'd worn to the first opening of the Biltmore?

"I wouldn't have worn black, would I? It was a joyous occasion—and the service was excellent." Then she added: "It all happened so quickly. I have no regrets. It wasn't easy—but it certainly was interesting."

Ghosts

HALFWAY through the process of paying attention to the Biltmore's past I became possessed with a need to climb up to the Tower to see what was there. I wanted to look down and up and around from this vantage point.

Granted, I'd been to that press conference for the Duke and Duchess of Windsor in the Tower suite back in the early 1940s and thought I remembered the occasion clearly. Memory being the tricky business it is, I had visualized two carved rock fireplaces instead of one, which fact I realized when I once again made it to the top.

Writing with exuberance of the 1926 opening of the Biltmore in the *Miami Riviera*, John V. Watts called attention to the "express elevator service which made the royal suites accessible to the main lobby. . . ." I am here to report there are stairs and stairs to climb after you reach the "royal suites," and the "express elevator service" ends before the top of the Tower is reached, that is, if your intention is to inspect the lights and walk around the parapet.

The last flights of steps are reminiscent of a castle in Wales, and somewhere about then I began to realize why the notion of a ghost inhabiting the Biltmore would have had to be invented to go with the Tower.

The rumor is that the ghost of a shabby gangster, one Fats Walsh, is known to prowl the upper regions of the Biltmore following his murder over a gambling debt.

The idea of a ghost appeals to people and appears to stimulate the imagination. While we were waiting to descend to the Grill one recent evening, the elevator button seemed unwilling to serve its purpose. Called on for assistance, an attendant led

Flying Ghost? The incomparable Ray Bolger in action.

us to a second elevator with a smile and a suggestion that "the ghost" had something to do with it.

I choose to dismiss the ghost of Fats Walsh as a fabrication but there is no doubt in my mind that ghosts do roam the corridors of the restored Biltmore. How could it be otherwise?

Would you accept Ray Bolger, the dancingest of men who graced the dinner shows and brought down the house with his golf routine back in the days of his youth? The day after the Preservation Ball to mark the second opening of the Biltmore after sixty-one years, I read of his death. It easily could have occurred as we were having our demitasses. I feel certain he would want to pay a return flying visit from time to time.

Ghosts are nudging my elbow as I write this: the diminutive Gladys Parker, who cloned herself in the cartoon *Flapper Fanny*, for instance. She presented a fashion show at the Biltmore, then tossed her creations into the arms of a bride-to-be as a gift. (I was the bride.)

No doubt Lord and Lady Mountbatten have bigger and better places to haunt but the image of them, squeezed into one telephone booth to accept a call from London, lingers in the atmosphere.

If at first you don't succeed, try, try, again. The redoubt-able David Dwight Eisenhower having trouble with his short pitches at the green at Pratt General Hospital.

Henri Germanini, a waiter in white gloves in the early days of the Biltmore, who left to serve as lifetime steward for the century old Biscayne Bay Yacht Club, would surely want to look in on things?

And how about President Eisenhower? No doubt he'd sooner haunt the Pentagon but, then, there is always that golf course as an enticement.

Perhaps the young and boisterous Johnny Weissmuller streaking down the corridors banging Bermuda doors would care to make a re-entry?

Finally, who could possibly deny the presence of George Merrick and, particularly while standing in the middle of his empty offices in the Giralda Tower?

In those rooms, looking out the window, I thought of George Merrick. Maybe that's one of the reasons I had to climb those cement flights of stairs in the Giralda Tower in order to see what he saw. Perhaps, to think about how it was the day he closed the door on it all.

Did he look back?

Probably not. His style was to move forward.

It does seem likely, however, that he would consider returning from other worlds to inspect the Biltmore now that it is so magnificently restored.

I looked out his window, surveying the scene as he once did, and what I saw would have pleased him. Down below, Tony Randall was making a movie.

The Biltmore was assuming its intended place in the world.

Later, walking around the open section at the top of the Tower, I thought of a sixty-nine year old yacht builder who as a child had a private clubhouse up there for his small-boy cronies.

Maybe that's another reason I wanted to go and look—to see where the "secret meetings" actually did take place.

When I reported I'd made the climb, Jack Ott asked immediately: "Did you climb the ladder?" I was ashamed to say I had stopped short of those threatening final steps. It seemed to please him that his secret meeting place was still a secret.

Full of the subject, I ran into artists Jill Cannaday and her husband, Robert Sindelir, and learned they had made the climb back in the 1970s when their hope to secure the Biltmore for an Arts Center motivated the exploration.

To my surprise, I learned that Dr. Jean Jones Perdue, the highly-regarded physician who has won national honors for her work in the heart field and with the elderly, once slept up in the Tower. She was ministering to Colonel Doherty during one of his bouts of ill health. Being new in the medical group with which she was associated during the 1930s, she caught the night work.

I had been present to observe some of the parade of characters at the Biltmore over a period of time, written about some, heard of others. They were a colorful lot, both the quick and the dead.

None more so than the man who had his heart set on bringing grandeur to the tomato patch he tended as a boy.

Merrick's passion for the Hispanic brought him a medal from the King of Spain, Alfonso XIII, but he never was free to accept an invitation to visit. Things were happening too fast at home. The medal rested for more than half a century on the ivory inlaid desk he carried out of the Tower and brought home to Eunice when he lost the Biltmore. It is our sad duty to report that it was stolen a few years ago. But the desk remains. Eunice uses it on which to write notes and open mail.

Other things remain as well, such as the poem called "Returning Alone," in which a loving husband visiting New York and missing Eunice, writes: *"But we dreamed it all true/ 'Twas real for us two."*

It turns out now that the Biltmore was real and stands today, a symbol of hope providing a happy ending for all of us.

Isn't that reason enough for George Merrick to be considered Ghost number one or *Numero Uno*, as we prefer to say in Hispanic-transformed Miami?

History has come full circle and caught up with George Merrick.

Acknowledgments

First I wish to thank Mrs. George Merrick for her unfailing patience as I questioned her. I can hear her saying, "It was a busy time. I can't ever remember George complaining."

Next I wish to thank Mildred Merrick, Richard's widow, who made available family history and papers including the financial record George kept on the motor trip the brothers took to the West Coast following the collapse of the boom.

A valued librarian at the University of Miami Library, her assistance provided extra dimension.

My thanks go to Mildred Crowe Langner, retired director of the University of Miami School of Medicine Library, for permitting me to read passages for checking; to Polly Dillon for sending material from that library; and to Joan Morris of the Florida State Archives for the many courtesies extended in Tallahassee.

The Miami Dade Public Library has long provided me with a second home, and in this instance for this work I wish to thank Sam Boldrick and Tom Milledge of the Florida Room for providing photographs from the Gleason Waite Romer Collection, as well as general information and material; to Director Edward F. Sintz, Assistant Director Marguerite Carden, and Lillian Baker, executive secretary, for constant assistance.

I appreciate the efforts of Becky Smith at the Historical Association of Southern Florida, and my thanks go as well to David A. Porfiri for allowing me to read his paper, "The Miami Biltmore Hotel and Country Club: A Monument to Memory."

Back in 1952 when I was working on *Miami USA* (Henry Holt 1953), I counted heavily on Miami newspapers for my material in addition to interviewing. It was the same this time, except for the fact that in 1987 the task is made much simpler by subsequent publications in the field and particularly the work of Howard Kleinberg, editor of The *Miami News.*

He began in the Spring of 1981 with a Saturday feature called "Miami: The Way We Were." By dipping into the files of The *Miami Metropolis,* forerunner of the *News* and Miami's first newspaper, he provides readers with a weekly on-the-spot coverage of events before the City of Miami was even incorporated.

Now in book form, and enhanced by additional information, this compilation doesn't just make researchers' lives easier, it makes the entire community richer. I appreciate the extra cooperation given me by Mr. Kleinberg, both with photographs and information available through the pages of the *News.*

There has been a blossoming of authentic historical material since I wrote *Miami USA,* with Arva Moore Parks and Thelma Peters emerging as diligent researchers and writers. Their works are listed under the Bibliography along with Mr. Kleinberg's.

Arva Parks has been more than generous on the occasions when I have appealed to her with a need for explanation. People have different recollections, and Arva and Thelma are in the front lines matching one against the other.

There is a long list of individuals whom I wish to mention beginning with Lyla Gorman Dix, one of the first people I met in December 1934 when I came to Miami with Carl Byoir Associates. She shared common impressions and jogged my memory on numerous occasions during the writing of this work.

In addition I appreciate my conversations with Becky Matkov, Keith W. Phillips, Jr., Charles J. Baldwin, Maggie and Leon Black, Petsy Mezey, Barbara Ashe, Dr. Nancy L. Noble, Jack Ott, Mrs. Hillard Willis, Richard Rose, Robert L. Koeppel, Jane Wood Reno, Jackson Hall Lewis, Gertrude Kent, Johanna Hoehl, Inman Padgett, Mary Lou Braznell, Phyllis Buhler, Dr. James Hutson, Lester Pancoast, and my old friend Thomas McE. Johnston, and for the many times I consulted with Leona Cayton, cousin of Eunice Merrick's and with Ellen Ugucionni, historic preservation admistrator of the City of Coral Gables.

I thank Edward Millstone for bringing his scrapbooks to the downtown library for me to peruse and Loretta Sheehy for sharing memories of the 1920s; also of inestimable help was Donald

Lebrun, City Manager of Coral Gables, who knows all about the Biltmore transactions from the moment it was turned back to Coral Gables and before.

I wish to thank all those other eager individuals who when they learned I was embarked on this undertaking came forward with reminiscences of the Biltmore in its many stages.

Finally, a salute to Charity Johnson, editor of The Pickering Press, who made the undertaking a happy experience.

Bibliography

Abbott, Carl P. *Open For The Season*. Doubleday, 1950.

Allen, Frederick Lewis. *Only Yesterday*. Harper & Row, 1931.

Antrim, Louanne S.; Chase, Charles Edwin; Ormond, Mark; Spring, Michael; Wilkins, Woodrow W. *The Biltmore Revisited*. Metropolitan Museum and Art Center, August 28 October 26, 1981.

Ashley, Kathryne. *George E. Merrick And Coral Gables, Florida*. Crystal Bay Publishers, Coral Gables, FL, 1985.

Ballinger, Kenneth. *Miami Millions*. The Franklin Press, 1936.

Beach, Rex. *The Miracle of Coral Gables*. Currier and Harford, Ltd., New York, 1926.

Caplan, Dr. Milton, and Marsh, Dr. Homer. "An Account of the Birth and Organization of the University of Miami School of Medicine." 1972.

Douglas, Marjory Stoneman. *Florida: The Long Frontier*. Harper & Row, 1967.

Dunlop, Beth. "Six Decades Old, Jewel of the Gables Is Sparkling Again." *The Miami Herald*, January 18, 1987.

Freeman, Susan Hale. "Monument to three Artists." *UPDATE.* Historical Association of Southern Florida, August, 1987.

Hiller, Herbert L. *Guide To The Small And Historic Lodgings Of Florida.* Pineapple Press, 1986.

Kleinberg, Howard. *Miami: The Way We Were. Miami Daily News,* 1985.

Parks, Arva Moore. *Miami: The Magic City.* Continental Heritage Press, 1981.

Peters, Thelma. *Biscayne Country 1870-1926.* Banyan Books, 1981.

Peterson, Susan. "Stars Glistened in Biltmore Watershows." *UPDATE.* Historical Association of Southern Florida, August, 1987.

Redford, Polly. *Billion-Dollar Sandbar.* E. P. Dutton, 1970.

Smiley, Nixon. *Yesterday's Miami.* E. A. Seemann Publishing, Inc., 1979.

Tebeau, Charlton W. *A History of Florida.* University of Miami Press, 1971.

Weigall, T. H. *Boom In Paradise.* Alfred H. King, 1932.

Werne, Jo. "He Does It All." *Historical Preservation Magazine.* (May/June 1987).

Werne, Jo. "Grandmother's Home Inspired Decorator of Hotel's Guests Rooms." *The Miami Herald,* January 18, 1987.

Wood, Prunella. "The Biltmore Debuts." *UPDATE.* Historical Association of Southern Florida, April, 1975.

Index